Meditation Techniques for Your Mental Health and to Connect to Your Angels

A Beginners' Guide to Meditating With Your Angels

Dawn Hazel

logo?

© Copyright 2022 - All rights reserved.

The content contained within this book may not be reproduced, duplicated or transmitted without direct written permission from the author or the publisher.

Under no circumstances will any blame or legal responsibility be held against the publisher, or author, for any damages, reparation, or monetary loss due to the information contained within this book, either directly or indirectly.

Legal Notice:

This book is copyright protected. It is only for personal use. You cannot amend, distribute, sell, use, quote or paraphrase any part, or the content within this book, without the consent of the author or publisher.

Disclaimer Notice:

Please note the information contained within this document is for educational and entertainment purposes only. All effort has been executed to present accurate, up to date, reliable, complete information. No warranties of any kind are declared or implied. Readers acknowledge that the author is not engaged in the rendering of legal, financial, medical or professional advice. The content within this book has been derived from various sources. Please consult a licensed professional before attempting any techniques outlined in this book.

By reading this document, the reader agrees that under no circumstances is the author responsible for any losses, direct or indirect, that are incurred as a result of the use of the information contained within this document, including, but not limited to, errors, omissions, or inaccuracies.

Table of Contents

INTRODUCTION 1
   ABOUT MEDITATION 2
      A Brief History of Meditation 2
      Benefits of Meditation 3
   ABOUT ANGELS 4
      Spiritual Guides and Helpers 4
   WHY DO MEDITATION AND ANGELS WORK SO WELL TOGETHER? 5
   HOW TO GET STARTED WITH THE NINE FORMS OF MEDITATION IF YOU'RE A BEGINNER OR RETURNING TO MEDITATION? 6
      Creating a Space 6
      Clearing the Energy in That Space 9
      When You Can't Create a Space, Try This 9

CHAPTER 1: BEGIN WITH YOUR MIND 11
   WHAT DOES MINDFULNESS MEDITATION INVOLVE? 12
      Acceptance of the Moment 12
      Awareness is Key 12
      Releasing Judgment and Self-Judgment 14
   BREATHWORK TO CENTER AND CALM 15
      Benefits of Breathwork 15
   WHEN TO DO MINDFULNESS MEDITATION AND EXERCISES 16
   TRY THIS: MEET YOUR ANGELS IN A MINDFULNESS MOMENT 16
      Let us begin this mindfulness meditation to connect to our angels around us now. 18

CHAPTER 2: BRING IN SOME ENERGY 23
   WHAT IS SPIRITUAL AND ENERGY-CLEARING MEDITATION? 24
   SPIRITUAL MEDITATION 25
      Getting the best out of Spiritual Meditation 25
      Practicing Spiritual Meditation at Home 26
   ENERGY-CLEARING MEDITATION 26
      When to do it? 27
      Do I Need to Believe in Chakras for It to Work? 27
   TRY THIS: ANGEL ENERGY-CLEARING MEDITATION 27
      Golden Light and Energy Clearing Meditation with Your Angels 29

CHAPTER 3: CHOOSE YOUR FOCUS 35

WHAT IS FOCUS MEDITATION 35
HOW DOES IT RELIEVE STRESS? 36
WHAT CAN I FOCUS ON?..37
TRY THIS: CALLING IN A SPECIFIC ANGEL THROUGH FOCUSED MEDITATION.......37
   Focus Meditation to Call in An Angel: Archangel Raphael for Healing........39

CHAPTER 4: MOVE IN A NEW DIRECTION 41

WHAT IS MOVEMENT MEDITATION? 41
TYPES OF MOVEMENT MEDITATION 41
TIPS OF MOVEMENT MEDITATION...42
TRY THIS: MOVEMENT MEDITATION AND HEALING FROM THE ANGELS.............44
   A Walking Meditation With Angel Healing 45

CHAPTER 5: DISCOVER YOUR MANTRA 49

WHAT IS MANTRA MEDITATION? 49
CAN I MAKE MY OWN MANTRA? 50
   Create Your Own Mantras and Affirmations..50
   Tips on Chanting Your Mantras 52
WHAT ARE MALA BEADS AND DO I NEED THEM? 53
TRY THIS: ANGEL PROTECTION/HEALING AND MANTRAS FOR TIMES OF EXTREME ANXIETY..54
   Angel Protection and Healing Meditation with Mantras for Times of Extreme Anxiety..55

CHAPTER 6: TIME TO CONSIDER TRANSCENDENCE 59

WHAT IS TRANSCENDENTAL MEDITATION? 59
   A Brief History of Transcendental Meditation 60
   Controversies 60
DOES IT WORK? 61
HOW DO I LEARN TRANSCENDENTAL MEDITATION? 62
   What to Expect During Your Transcendental Meditation Course................62

CHAPTER 7: PROGRESS A LITTLE FURTHER 63

WHAT IS PROGRESSIVE MEDITATION?..63
HOW IS A BODY SCAN DIFFERENT?...63
WHAT DO I NEED TO SUCCESSFULLY DO A PROGRESSIVE MEDITATION?..........64
TRY THIS: BODY SCAN AND PROGRESSIVE MEDITATION WITH THE ANGELS TO HELP HEAL YOUR INNER CHILD 65
   Body Scan and Progressive Meditation with the Angels to Help Heal Your Inner Child..67

CHAPTER 8: AMPLIFY THE GOOD VIBES 73

WHAT IS A LOVING-KINDNESS AND COMPASSION MEDITATIONS? 73
DOES IT HELP ME, TOO?..74
HOW TO DO A LOVING-KINDNESS MEDITATION 75

TRY THIS: LOVING-KINDNESS MEDITATION WITH THE EARTH ANGELS 77
Loving-Kindness Meditation to Help Heal the Earth and A Difficult Situation *78*

CHAPTER 9: CREATE YOUR NEW VISIONS 83

WHAT IS VISUALIZATION? 83
HOW CAN I USE IT IN MEDITATION? 84
TIPS FOR VISUALIZATION 85
TRY THIS: VISUALIZING A PATH FORWARD WITH ANGEL GUIDANCE 86
Visualization with Angel Help to Find the Best Path Forward *87*

CHAPTER 10: CONNECT TO YOUR HIGHER SELF 93

WHY CONNECT TO MY HIGHER SELF? 93
WHY SHOULD I HAVE ANGELIC PROTECTION WHEN SPEAKING TO MY HIGHER SELF? 94
TRY THIS: CONVERSATION WITH YOUR HIGHER SELF IN A SAFE SPACE 95
Meditation for a Conversation With Your Higher Self in a Safe Space *96*

CONCLUSION 101

KEEP IN MIND 102
ADDITIONAL TIPS FOR MEDITATION 104
TIPS FOR HOSTING GROUP MEDITATIONS 105
MORE ABOUT ANGELS 107

REFERENCES 109

IMAGES 118

Introduction

Few have not picked up a book about meditation, and read through it with grand ideas of a changed lifestyle, only to close the cover and forget all about it. Meditation seems to be one of those things that are easier to read about than actually *do*.

It takes time to learn, to get into the groove of practicing regularly, refine techniques, and begin seeing lasting results. There's no need to feel bad about it. So many of us are time-strapped and have a million things we need to do, to remember, to attend to before the day is out.

But what if meditation is the way for you to strike three things off your list in one go. What if meditation could, in addition to providing health benefits and creative inspiration, also connect you to your spiritual guides—your angels—whenever you choose.

What if setting aside that 15–20 minutes a day, or every two days, for some quiet me-time strengthened your spiritual body and your emotional healing. What if that same time could be used to interact with your angels and receive healing, love, and guidance from them.

All these what-ifs can become reality, but that depends on you. How willing are you to step out of your comfort zone? How willing are you to develop a new habit that involves meditation and visualization?

In the time that it takes you to drink a cup or two of hot coffee each day (we're not counting the ones that turn into frappes when you get stuck into doing something else), you can get the three-fold benefit of meditating with your angels. There's only one thing to remember when you first begin meditating and that's it's going to take time and a little bit of perseverance. The rest you'll learn and figure out as we go along.

Before we dive into meditation practices and techniques, let's get a little grounding on meditation, the angels, and some things we can do to turn our meditation time into a quality multi-purpose session.

About Meditation

Meditation at its core is all about disconnecting from conscious thoughts and distractions in the physical world. In the past, it would also be referred to as Contemplation. The likelihood that you've already naturally experienced a meditative moment is quite high.

Maybe it's that time you sat outside in the sun and listened to the birds, or watched the butterflies dance without once picking up your phone or thinking about what's for dinner. Maybe it's that time you "spaced out" after a twelve-hour shift and felt so relaxed that you fell asleep as soon as your head hit the pillow.

So, what makes regular meditation practice so difficult? One reason may be that it's scary to consciously disconnect! What if you miss a call or a text? What if you disconnect from your body and can't get back? What if you sat there for half an hour and *nothing* significant happened and it feels like wasted time?

It's normal and healthy to have these questions. Now that we've acknowledged some of the fears and concerns about meditation, let's have a lightning tour through the history of meditation and then move on to the benefits.

A Brief History of Meditation

Most modern meditation practices stem from Eastern meditation practices stretching back several thousand years. However, many other cultures and their shamans also practice forms of meditation to access deeper or alternative states of being.

The first written mentions of meditations are from Jainism, but the ones we most commonly encounter and practice evolved from Hinduism and Buddhism (Wikipedia, 2019). Other cultures also practice spiritual and religious meditations: Judaism, Christianity, Islam, and several other religions.

From the mid to late 18th century, Asian meditation was introduced to the West. It gained in popularity while, during a cultural exchange of ideas, it reignited interest in Western meditative practices.

Increased interest and practice in related or 'new' meditation techniques and yoga from the 1960s through to the 1980s (the New Age Movement) brought meditation into mainstream culture and made it more accessible to everyone.

Benefits of Meditation

Scientific research on the benefits and effects of meditation and meditation techniques have often reinforced personal experiences and anecdotes. Interest continues to grow in meditation as a self-care routine.

Most meditation techniques tend to reduce stress and alleviate depression. By calming the mind and soothing the nervous system, regular meditation can also benefit your heart and other organs as well as relieve anxiety. Most people find that more than one technique works well for them, so reaping the widest range of benefits for their health (Burke et al, 2017).

About Angels

While the term angels are often thought of in a religious context, today the term can be applied to our spiritual guides and helpers from all spheres, religions, and cultures. Most angels are always around to guide, comfort, and provide aid whenever you give them permission to do so. Anyone can call on them or work with them when in need and when your intentions are aligned to healing, empowering, and seeking or providing support.

Spiritual Guides and Helpers

As your spiritual guides and helpers, angels are present to support you emotionally, spiritually, and sometimes practically through advice, counseling, and their own brand of magic or miracles. Your angels can be guides and protectors from birth, celestial beings such as archangels, and angels with specific niches.

We know of parking angels and kitchen angels, and yes! Sales and finance angels, too! These high-vibration teammates and friends in spirit never brush off your fears and frailties. However, they will only intervene with your permission. It's important to remember that angels are beings who take boundaries seriously. They will never take away your free will.

Why Do Meditation and Angels Work So Well Together?

Angels' messages and communication, such as angel numbers and signs, can often be missed in the hectic dealings of your typical day. When in meditation, your mind is less preoccupied and is more open to the present. In other words, it's easier for angels to catch your attention and convey a message.

Another reason angels and meditation work so well together is that during meditations, your body is relaxed and your ego less (or not) in charge of things. Your mind and heart are more aligned. This makes healings and alignments easier to achieve.

How to Get Started with the Nine Forms of Meditation if You're a Beginner or Returning to Meditation?

While it may be daunting to imagine starting a meditation session by yourself, or maybe you feel you don't have the time, there is a way to minimize things so it's no longer a block. Naturally, choosing a meditation is crucial as it will determine where and how you do it, but for the majority of techniques creating a space helps you settle into the process of meditating with less difficulty and makes for a more pleasant experience.

Creating a Space

The size of the space you choose makes no difference. You can do it in a tiny space or the great outdoors. The most important aspect of your meditation space is the atmosphere. Quiet and a sense of harmony are also factors that need to be considered.

Atmosphere

You need to be comfortable in the atmosphere of the room or area you will be meditating in. Consider the temperature, the smells and sounds around you, the flow of air, and especially how relaxed you feel in that space. Any aspect that creates dissonance for you can be tempered or a new space can be found if it's outdoors.

If a space is too cool or hot, it can break your meditation or change your experience. If you're indoors and have air conditioning, you may want to adjust it to a suitable temperature. Most people tend to grow chilled, even in summer, when meditating for more than ten minutes, so you may want to keep an extra throw or rug handy.

Some like to burn incense or use scent diffusers to nullify smells or to enhance a room. This isn't necessary unless you like incense. If, however, you're sensitive to smoke or tend to lose track of time, it's best to avoid strong incense and burners. Some incense burners can pose a fire hazard, so take precautions to ensure your safety. Room sprays are another alternative that is easy to use anyplace and can still create the same effect.

Quiet

Noisy environments and those filled with harsh sounds are notorious for ruining a good meditation session! The time of day often makes a huge difference to the noises and sounds around. Even in the countryside, the sound of a tractor or a buzzsaw can be distracting.

At home, in usually noisy neighborhoods, early morning can be the quietest time to meditate. In certain cultures, 4 a.m. to 6 a.m. is considered one of the most auspicious times to meditate, but if that isn't possible for you, you can note the typical noises of your neighborhood and choose the best times for you.

Music, whether through earbuds or earphones, or gently playing in the background can also help counter distracting environmental sounds and give you a focus for your meditation! Choose instrumental tracks that are repetitive and calming to yourself. If you find yourself preferring mantras, then a mantra track can also be used.

Harmony

Atmosphere and quiet can help produce harmony within your space, and so too does what many describe as the energy of the place. This will either make you feel comfortable, neutral, or uncomfortable.

For example, if you're sitting in a room where every time you close your eyes you find yourself distracted or feeling watched or just restless, it could be that the energies aren't harmonious with yours. If you feel comfortable, relaxed, and safe within the space, then it's most likely that you and the space are in harmony. For this reason, clearing your meditation space energetically, or consecrating it in some way—

making it holy in your mind—helps you feel connected and safe and also allows you to experience your angels without interference.

Clearing the Energy in That Space

A simple cleansing ritual and intention are all that are usually needed to clear the energy in a space. One of the easiest ways to do this is to set up an energetic circle that filters out lower vibrations and contains positive vibes. Some choose to use crystals, oils, and incense or even consecrate the space in the name of a deity or other powerful benevolent being, or, most often with the Archangels: Michael, Raphael, Gabriel, and Uriel.

When You Can't Create a Space, Try This

Visualize a circle of golden light before you begin each session, then center yourself. The beauty of this last method is that you can clear the energy in any space without impacting others through scents, chanting, or dishonoring a space that might be sacred to a tribe already. By centering yourself in a bubble of love and light, you are also grounding yourself and securing yourself in a positive energy.

Alternatively, you can carry a stone such as black tourmaline, onyx, or obsidian plus rose quartz or clear quartz to cleanse the energy in the area immediately around you.

Chapter 1:

Begin with Your Mind

One of the biggest blocks most people find to developing a meditation habit is a preconception they hold about the practice or requirements of meditation. Things like: you need to clear your mind of all thoughts, you need to sit in a lotus position, you need to have a special area or special clothes, or you need to worship a specific deity or follow a different religion. While certain meditation schools may have these requirements, most don't.

We invite you to sit down, set aside your preconceptions, and give mindfulness meditation a try. This technique has grown enormously in popularity for its do-it-anytime-anywhere approach and for its health benefits. Studies have compared levels of hypertension in groups practicing mindfulness meditation to those who do not (Ponte Márquez, et al.).

After eight weeks the mindfulness meditation group had shown a decrease in their overall blood pressure levels. They also reported lower instances of being judgmental and feeling less depressed. Mindfulness meditation can also help in pain management, relieving stress and anxiety, reducing or remedying insomnia, and increasing memory retention and improved focus. Clarity is a goal that many achieve through mindfulness meditations.

What Does Mindfulness Meditation Involve?

Mindfulness Meditation is a technique used to 'quieten' the mind by shifting your awareness from your thoughts to the world around you, a sound or mantra, or even a tiny detail of your world.

Acceptance of the Moment

If you can get the hang of accepting the moment, you'll have mindfulness meditation down pat! Also called "being in the moment," mindfulness meditation seeks to draw your attention away from the millions of everyday thoughts you have. It seeks to hit the pause or skip button and to provide you with a mental and spiritual space to just *be*. Being in the moment without worry, without planning for a future event or maybe event, without agonizing over relationships or the finances. It's the ultimate me-time.

Awareness is Key

Entering the state of "being in the moment" is not as difficult as it sounds. Shifting your awareness unlocks a calmness that brings clarity and greater conscious choice on where to shift your attention and awareness next.

You may want to experiment with various ways to achieve that calm, aware state. Try concentrating on a sound: the sound of the breeze in the trees, the trickle or drip of water, or the hum of the air conditioning. If you like music, you can listen to a restful or calming track with a distinct rhythm or beat that is repetitive. The repetitiveness is what will calm you down and keep you in the moment. Instrumental music is best as lyrics are likely to distract you.

Another method of shifting your awareness that may appeal to you is to focus on a sensation. You may want to feel into the warmth of the sun on your face or your palms, the coziness of your jumper or a throw, or the brush of your hair every time an oscillating fan changes direction.

Another way to focus on the moment is to close your eyes and catalog the smells and scents in your environment. But be careful with this one! It can be distracting at times, too!

A method that takes some practice but is worth the effort is to close your eyes and focus on the space directly in front of your eyes. You may hear a jumble of thoughts and that's okay. You may also see orange dots or forms, or violet ones. That's perfectly normal, too. Soon, you'll find your thoughts are clearer and your body more relaxed.

Releasing Judgment and Self-Judgment

Releasing judgment and self-judgment makes this meditation easier to achieve. In practice, this means that when thoughts arise, you acknowledge them if you'd like then let them go. Don't get stuck on what others think about you sitting still for 15 minutes, or berate yourself for not stopping the flow of thoughts.

Everyone's thought about the thing they forgot to do just before the meditation session or how much they need the restroom! This is why it's best to always take a comfort break before you begin meditating. But don't judge yourself for forgetting to do so, either.

In time, you'll see this less judgmental side of yourself grow and ease the tension in your life. As an additional bonus, your self-love will be greater and more easily expressed as well.

Breathwork to Center and Calm

Breathwork is simply taking deliberate, well-spaced breaths or breathing to a prescribed rhythm. It's also paying attention to your breathing and the effect it is having on your body. For example, on an in-breath, you may feel the flow of air through your nostril, hear your intake, and experience the expanding of your lungs and the rise of your chest. Certain kinds of breathwork can sometimes make you feel giddy.

Benefits of Breathwork

Awareness of breath stops the incessant turntable of your thoughts. If you don't have music or other sounds available to focus on, or if they make you feel uncomfortable, your own breath works just as well to quiet your mind. Concentrating on your breathing rhythm is almost instantly calming and changing that rhythm holds your brain's attention, drowning out most thoughts or relegating them to insignificant.

Give it a try now if you're feeling anxious. Take a deep breath, then slowly let it out through your nostrils. Again. And once again. No paper bag needed. Some people call this centering. Others call it being fully in your body.

Breathwork is great for relaxing your muscles. If you typically have your shoulders hunched up when stressed, during breathwork, you will notice that after a few breaths, your shoulders relax and so do your face muscles. Your internal muscles ease as well and some may feel the shape or tension in their stomach change as well.

Breathwork allows you to consciously choose what you wish to focus on. Once the flow of thoughts is eased by breathwork, you have the clarity and presence of mind to consciously choose what you'd like to deliberate on. It could be what's for dinner or how to solve the housing problem. For others, it's a great way to start a <u>visualization</u>.

When to Do Mindfulness Meditation and Exercises

You can do a mindfulness meditation at almost any time that doesn't involve you driving/steering a vehicle, caring for another (unless they join you), attending meetings, and when you feel unsafe in a neighborhood.

For example, during household chores, eating, disconnecting from your social networks, and turning off your devices.

Try This: Meet Your Angels in a Mindfulness Moment

In this introduction to your angels, we're going to create a safe space, go into a state of mindfulness or meditation, then request our angels around us to make themselves known. We're also going to request a sign that indicates that our angels are sending us a message or that they are with us. During this part of the meditation, you may be given signs traditionally regarded as angelic—white feathers, images of angels or angel wings, the chime of bells to name a few—or a sign unique for yourself.

With a little practice, you can soon drop into this meditation and speak to your angels as often as you wish.

Allow 15 to 20 minutes for this meditation. If this is the first time you're doing it, allow 30 to 35 minutes. You can have someone read it out to you, or you can record yourself reading it through to the end. Allow time for the messages to be received and signs to be given.

To begin, you'll need to sit or lie in a position that will be comfortable for you over the next 20 minutes. Loosen any tight clothing and shoes, mute your devices, and let people know you're unavailable for the next half hour or so. When you're ready, settle down and we'll proceed. First, we'll create a safe space. Next, we'll do some breathwork, then connect to our angels. We'll end by closing the meditation in the same way that we began.

Let us begin this mindfulness meditation to connect to our angels around us now.

Are you sitting comfortably? Notice the texture beneath you, the flow of air on your face, and the instances of cold and heat over different parts of your body. Notice them. That's all that's required.

Are random or familiar thoughts clambering for your attention? Give in to them for a split second then let them go. Allow them to flow off into the day, acknowledged and ready to be attended to in good time. Allow your mind and your body some breathing space. For now, this time is yours to relax, just be, and to eventually communicate with the highest frequency angels around you if you so wish.

We're going to create a circle: a bubble that holds nothing but the highest frequencies, a filter that sifts out tension and low densities and converts them into the love and light of the highest available frequencies.

When you're ready, close your eyes and see yourself sitting there. A golden beam of light, like a laser pen, appears. Direct it to draw a circle clockwise, left-hand to right-hand, and back again. Make it so this curtain of golden light only filters in the best for you: the highest vibrations, the most healing experiences, and the greatest love while converting all tension and lower densities into the highest forms of light and love.

When you're done, keep your eyes closed. Know that you are safe and secure within this circle, and that you control what enters and exits it. At all times, this circle of light is purifying and transmuting energies in and around it to the highest vibrations possible.

You're going to take three deep breaths. Breathing in through your nose and breathing out through your mouth. If this doesn't work for you, you can breathe through your nostrils only.

Ready? Breathe in slowly. There is no rush. Breathe out slowly. Notice how calm and relaxed you're feeling. Breathe in again, slowly, slowly.

Breathe out again even slower. Let's do this one more time. Notice how serene you feel. Enjoy this feeling. If you wish to pause here for a minute or two to enjoy this calm, please do so.

It's time to connect to our heart by dropping into it. Take a moment to consider your mind's eye. It's open while your physical eyes are closed.

In your mind's eye, see your heart open. You may see it open like a book, or maybe a flower blossoming. There is no right or wrong way for it to open. Watch your beautiful, big heart open, glowing brighter and brighter as it does. What color is your heart? Watch its glow spread and envelope you from head to toe like a cozy blanket. Watch your heart's light expand even further to a hand's length around you, then to double that length beyond you. Your heart is now open. Breathe in deeply, then out slowly. Repeat.

Now that we're safe and our hearts are open, we're ready to meet our angels. There is nothing to fear. Your angels are all around you and ready to assist whenever you ask.

Direct your attention back to the circle of light around you. We are now going to invite your angels into your circle to reveal themselves to you. To your circle of light say out loud or in your mind:

> *I invite my angels around me into this sacred space. I ask that they now send me any messages that I need or are ready to hear at this time. I thank them.*

With your eyes closed, listen. Keep breathing slowly and deeply. It is okay if you don't see anything in your mind's eye or hear anything at this time. Keep breathing. If you wish, you may repeat the invitation to your angels, but it is not necessary. Some may not experience an angel at first and that is okay. When the time is right, you will. Continue to relax and enjoy this space.

You may hear a pleasant voice in your mind speak to you. If they don't introduce themselves, ask their name. Be curious. You can speak to them as you would a new acquaintance. It need not be formal. If you prefer, you may ask to see with your mind's eye what your angel looks like. If your angel is not dressed with wings and white robes or the garments you'd expect, you can question them further.

Angels are infinitely patient and love answering questions and having discussions, although the answers and outcomes may not always be as expected! Angels have a good sense of humor and don't be afraid to share yours with them. Enjoy getting to know and befriending your angel.

If your angel has not yet given you a message, you may ask for one again. Listen, and if you need clarification, don't be afraid to ask for some.

When your conversation is winding down and your message has been received, ask your angel to give you a sign that a message in the physical world comes from them. In your mind's eye, your angel will show you this sign or allow you to experience it in some other way, such as a gentle brush against your cheek, a tingle in your fingertips, or lifting your hair. Your sign is tailored for you by your angels. It will be part of the natural world, but distinct at the same time. Treasure the gift of your sign and, if you have no more questions, thank your angels.

Your angel may disappear from your mind's eye at this stage or seem to retreat. Some may ask if you'd like them to stay with you a little longer. It's your choice.

Send love and thanks to your angels. You may experience an energetic hug or give one yourself if you feel called to.

Now, we'll take down the circle while retaining our open hearts and the highest frequencies of this meditation. We'll also remember the angel's message and the sign or signs we were given.

In your mind's eye, see a laser pen of pink light appear. We're going to trace over the golden circle with this pink light in a reverse direction. When you're ready, draw over the golden circle moving from right to left and completing the circle on your right-hand side. See the golden circle turn pink as you do so. Once you have completed the pink circle, watch it disperse in your mind's eyes. If you so wish, you can send love out into the world dispersing it as the circle disperses.

Notice the textures and feel of the environment around you. Feel your fingers and toes. Feel your lashes flutter. Open your eyes and take a deep breath.

You may wish to drink some water now and over the course of the next hour. Don't forget to write down your angel message and your angel sign. Watch for the sign over the next few days and now your angels are communicating with you even if it's only to remind you that they are there for you.

In your next meditation, you can carry on from where you left off, and discover the name and sign of another angel.

Remember to always put up your circle and to take it down. This way, you are only dealing with the highest frequencies of angels around you.

Chapter 2:

Bring in some Energy

If you're craving more ease and flow in your life, consider Spiritual and energy-clearing meditation.

Working with energy during meditation is powerfully healing, relaxing, and revitalizing. It may sound weird, but it's one of the most popular types of meditation that utilizes the scientific theory that everything is energy. Therefore, working with energy is a way of working on all aspects of yourself at once. You may wonder how you, a person, can work with energy.

Remember that you, as part of the universe, are an energetic being. It's why static electricity is such a problem! Light is also energy, so you can see it around you and use its behavior as a guide to visualizing and directing energy. So, while working with energy during meditation isn't likely to turn you into the next Merlin, it can still work wonders on your well-being. So can spiritual meditation.

What is Spiritual and Energy-Clearing Meditation?

Spiritual meditation, as the name suggests, seeks to explore yourself beyond your physical body and environment. It's the meditation of choice when a person wishes to connect to the divine. When someone says they are seeking their path or their truth, they're most likely to choose this form of meditation.

Spiritual meditation has two aspects to it. One can be seen as an extension of mindfulness into deep reflection, the other can be seen as a conscious action of connecting to your soul and a divine presence through prayers of invocation. Most religions practiced today have some form of spiritual meditation.

However, by practicing the aspect of spiritual meditation that is an extension of mindfulness into a personal journey of self-reflection, you don't have to subscribe to any religion or other belief systems. People who wish to know their soul better or to overcome some personal obstacles such as addictions or healing after great personal loss will often practice spiritual healing more than any other form of meditation (Burke, et al. 2017).

Spiritual meditation appeals to people seeking a sustainable way of helping themselves alleviate depression and other mental health issues. As more research is done, we continually get confirmation that this form of self-help and self-healing is beneficial to most individuals, no matter which aspect they choose to practice.

Energy meditation and healing is the practice of clearing your energetic fields using your mind and heart electromagnetic fields and stabilizing those fields. One method of energy clearing utilizes chakras—energy points in your body that are often thought to be the 'plug-in' points of your body and electric field. Another method is to use your central column or spine as the focus point. Yet another method, though less popular, is to enter a state of mindfulness, then envision everything around you, and eventually the universe, as pure energy.

Spiritual Meditation

Depending on your preference, spiritual meditation can be done in a group or in a solitary way. If you prefer a non-religious meditation, it would be best to check with your local meditation facilitators to ensure you'll be comfortable practicing with an established group. Ask if you can do a try-out before committing to any programs and expenses.

Exploring spiritual meditation in your home may need a little more preparation, but it's free, and you can choose methods that resonate fully with you.

Getting the best out of Spiritual Meditation

Begin without expectation. This allows you the openness to experience whatever comes to you in the moment. This approach may bring varying degrees of 'success' in terms of reaching revelations, but it cracks open the door for great self-understanding, sudden insights into the universe, and sometimes blissful, profound experiences. Each meditation is likely to be unique.

Be patient. Pushing to achieve some goal in spiritual meditation is like pushing a car while it's in park. It's a waste of energy. Keep in mind that the benefits will take time to appear and that the blissful and deeply spiritual experiences will only happen when you are ready to receive them.

Choose a time. Most practitioners do a morning session, or an evening session, although, if your schedule allows, you can do a meditation any time of the day. A morning meditation can help you set the tone for your day and keep you in a less reactive space. An evening meditation can relax you and help your sleep quality. A midday meditation can help you destress and alleviate anxiety about events you may have to attend in the evening.

Practicing Spiritual Meditation at Home

Prepare your space well. Pay attention to the cleansing of the area.

If your meditation is going to be devotional, gather an image and write out a prayer, memorize it, or have a book handy to read out loud. If you are using a chant or prayer that's in a language not native to you, practice pronunciation so you feel more confident in your invocation.

Energy-Clearing Meditation

There are many audio guided meditations that take you through energy clearing. Most follow a simple process of opening your heart, grounding, clearing each of the seven major chakra points, then bringing in fresh energy to heal and rejuvenate your electrical body.

Some guided meditations may also include additional energy healing or manifesting a goal. It is best to begin simply so that you get used to working with energy.

When to do it?

It's not recommended to do energy clearings daily if you are not in a safe space or out in public. Once the process is started it must be completed, so choose a time—maybe once a week to begin with—when you won't be disturbed for about 20 minutes to half an hour.

When you have some practice doing energy-clearing, you can do them when you're feeling ill, have continual negative experiences, or feel constantly drained and fatigued.

Do I Need to Believe in Chakras for It to Work?

You don't need to believe in chakras any more than you need to believe in your spleen or your thyroid gland. Chakras or energy centers in your body are theories and beliefs that cross cultures and religious beliefs. Most people find working with chakras intuitive and fairly easy.

If you'd prefer not to use the chakra methods, there is the column method. Instead of clearing and directing energy through each chakra point, you only work with the central column of light running along your spine. This incorporates all the energy centers without you working on them individually. While this may save some time, it may also take a little longer to analyze some aspects of your life or situation.

Try This: Angel Energy-Clearing Meditation

Angels are wonderful for helping with energy clearing and facilitating spiritual meditation. In the following meditation, we're going to focus solely on energy clearing. Before we begin, take a moment to notice if you're feeling tired, tense, overwrought over an idea, or confused about something (maybe a relationship). After the meditation, you can reassess these points. This will show you how responsive to energy-clearing you are.

Allow 15 to 20 minutes for each session. Avoid this meditation if you have taken alcohol up to about three hours before.

There is no need for incense or other enhancements unless you feel the ritual of lighting them will help you in concentrating.

It's best to do this meditation sitting instead of lying down.

We'll begin as we did for the mindfulness meditation. After calling in our angels, we will open our column of light and ground into Earth. Once grounded, we will clear our energy, bring in fresh energy and stabilize everything with the golden light. Please have some water at hand for directly after the meditation as you'll need to hydrate.

If at any time you feel uncomfortable stop with the energy-clearing, skip to the stabilizing with the golden light, and re-ground yourself before closing the meditation. Energy clearing can bring up long-held trauma. We may often cry or feel some overwhelm during an intense clearing or when we first begin this practice.

Other physical sensations may be felt, too, sometimes in your belly, other times on your face, above your head, and in your feet and hands. Energy can sometimes feel like a tingle or generate heat and cold in various spots of your body. Intense releases may also feel like prickly heat. It should soon pass. Everyone is different and experiences energy in their own unique way, so while these are the most well-known effects felt during energy healing, there may be other sensations that you may feel, too.

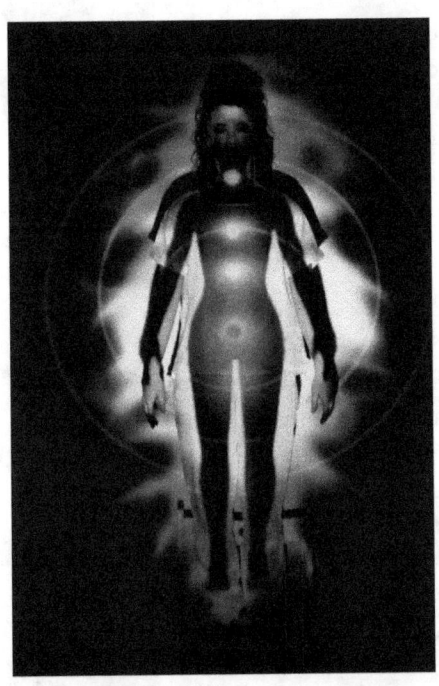

Golden Light and Energy Clearing Meditation with Your Angels

When you're sitting comfortably upright, we'll begin.

Take a deep breath and when you breathe out, release all tension and discomfort in your body. Notice your hands, your feet. Are your feet flush on the ground? Set your soles firmly on the ground and feel how they anchor you.

Take a deep breath and when you breathe out, release any niggly thoughts and judgments at this time. Either this process will work for you or it won't. All that matters now is that you are ready and willing to experience clearing your energy of any and all residues from your past.

Notice your arms and hands. Are they lying comfortably on your lap or your knees? Adjust them so that your open palms are either facing up or down. Avoid clenching your hands, but you may curl them if you so wish so that they are neither open nor closed.

Take another slow deep breath, breathing into your belly. Feel or watch it rise. Release all of your breath and watch your belly sink then rise again as you take another deep breath. Take as many breaths as you need or feel called to.

When you're ready, close your eyes.

See a pen of golden light appear. Direct it to draw a golden circle of light clockwise around you and the area you're in, the pen moving from 1 o'clock to 3 o'clock and all the way past 11 o'clock to complete the glowing circle. Once complete, this circle expands out so that it is now a bubble of light and you are at its center.

Fill this bubble up with only the highest frequencies of light and love, filtering out negativity, stress, and dense energies. Within your circle, you are calm and safe.

Now, we will call in the angels for further protection and to help us with our energetic house-clearing.

You may use these words or similar ones that feel natural to you:

> *I call on the highest frequency angels, and Archangels Michael, Gabriel, Uriel, and Raphael to help me hold this safe, sacred space at the highest frequencies of love and light. I ask for their help in clearing my energy of any and all dense energies, all blocks, and all energies that are no longer relevant to me. I thank them.*

You may see or feel the angels at this time as confirmation that they are present and ready to help you with the process. If you don't feel them or see them in your mind's eye, that is okay. They are still there and will still assist you.

It's time to begin the energy clearing. We will begin by opening our hearts as we have done before.

When you're ready, direct your attention to your area that is your heart. Feel it expand as it opens. See it in your mind's eye glowing brighter and brighter. What color is it? Watch the glow of light expand and wash all over you. See your heart's light expand in another bubble around you, about an arm's length from your body.

Take a breath and direct your attention to the space about a palm's height above your head. This is your crown chakra—the energy point that enables your constant connection to source, to god, to the universe, to all that is, and also to your most evolved and loving self.

When you're ready imagine a golden spotlight from the heart of the universe, from source, from the divine, shining down onto your crown. It illuminates a path all the way down your spinal column and continues down into the heart of the earth or Gaia. This is your column of light.

Take a deep breath and draw down the golden light through your skull, through your neck, and along your body, right down into the heart of the earth. Take another deep breath and see the golden light return from Gaia up your spinal column and into Source. With each breath you take, this exchange of energy grounds and nourishes you so any energy we clear is immediately replaced and so we avoid depletion.

Feel this golden light washing over your entire body and filling up the bubble of light you sit in. If you wish, you can expand this nourishing golden light out into your larger circle of light.

Now, see the golden spotlight infused with violet and silver light. Although it is light, it behaves like water—a gentle, warm, shower that washes and cleanses you. It washes over your face, your brain, and your nervous system. It clears your sinuses and all your electrical pathways, washing away all blocks, all dense energies, and all energetic gunk that accumulates.

The golden cleansing light with violet and silver light continues washing you, down past your throat, allowing you to speak with more clarity and less hesitancy, allowing you to clearly express yourself. The light continues down, purifying your heart and torso area where your solar plexus is. It cleanses all your organs, all your cells, and all the components of your cells to the smallest particles and the spaces in between.

The light swirls down past the small of your belly button and the small back—your root chakra that connects you to the earth, cleansing and purifying, gently clearing all trauma and frustration. The light rains down through your hands and feet and into the earth where it transmutes into the highest frequencies of love, joy, and nourishment.

You may sit in this gentle shower of light for as long as you wish, and when you are ready, notice that the light raining down now has seven additional beautiful colors: red, orange, yellow, green, blue, violet, and silver. As it rains down, these colors nourish you—your energy centers or chakras—and balance so that they settle into harmony within your body and energetic bodies.

If you wish, you can expand this multicolored waterfall of light so that it is nourishing and balancing your bubble and other circles of light. This waterfall of light is now a part of the processes that flow through your central column of light—cleansing and nourishing you, and doing the same for the earth and Gaia too.

We have done the major part of the clearing and it will continue to gently cleanse for a few hours more, but before we end, we'll ask our angels if there is any other clearing that we're ready to do. If you are in pain or have an ailment, you may request the angels to help you further shift and cleanse the areas that require more work.

Sit still and allow your angels to help you shift what is next needed to shift. Breath evenly as your angels work. You may feel sensations around your face or over your body. You may hear advice and guidance and receive reassurance and love, too.

When your angels are done or if there was no work to do, it's time to close the meditation.

Thank your angels. Thank your body, Thank the universe or Source. And send them all love.

In your mind's eye see the link between your spine hold securely to the heart of the earth and to the heart of Source as the golden light continually flows through. You are now grounded. Feel your feet sitting firmly on the ground.

Now, direct your attention to a pen of pink light. Use this pen to draw over the outer circle of golden light in an anti-clockwise direction—12 o'clock to 11 o'clock to 10 o'clock until you're back at 12 o'clock and the circle is entirely pink. Now, see this pink circle disperse and fade, sending love out into the universe.

Take a deep breath and shift your shoulders. Wiggle your toes and fingers. Yawn if you wish. And open your eyes if they are still closed.

How do you feel? What did you experience? Did your angels give you any advice?

You may want to journal to retain these answers. Compare them to your next (and previous) meditation.

All that is now needed to complete this energy clearing process is for you to hydrate. Warm water is best. Avoid coffee and tea for a little while, if possible.

If you would like to try adding chakras to this meditation for your next session, use this guide to locate the chakras in your body. As the waterfall of light runs through, imagine the chakras start to turn like waterwheels, picking up speed until they're spinning disks of light.

- *Crown chakra: white or gold*
- *Third Eye chakra: violet or silver*
- *Throat Chakra: blue*
- *Heart chakra: green*
- *Solar Plexus chakra: yellow*
- *Sacral chakra: orange*
- *Root chakra: red*

Chapter 3:

Choose Your Focus

Shift away from stress with a respite from your usual train of thought with a Focus Meditation. Also called Focused Attention Meditation or Concentrative Meditation, this cousin of the Mindfulness Meditation is a good way to practice stillness and detachment. It's also a good option when first starting a practice and if you are often distracted during meditation by never-ending thoughts.

Focus Meditation has been a part of meditation practice since time immemorial. Fixing attention on a fire or watching a stream comes naturally to most of us. Written history and texts suggest that Focus Meditation was practiced in ancient India along with open-awareness practices.

What is Focus Meditation

Focus Meditation is practiced by giving all of your attention to one object or subject. The aim of this meditation is to concentrate on the subject to the point that you become unaware of everything else but that subject. The purpose of this meditation is to increase concentration and mental abilities, but it also has the benefit of relieving stress and calming emotions.

How Does it Relieve Stress?

Focus Meditation trains your mind to observe and mute distractions in your environment. The stress relief factor is that you are less likely to be distracted by elements in your environment that would normally hinder your productivity and your emotional balance, for example, a dog barking incessantly in the background during a phone call.

You are less likely to react emotionally (yell at the dog), and more likely to find a happy solution (distract the dog with a treat or a scratch). Neither you nor the dog will be stressed out by the second scenario. This meditation practice can also help alleviate anxiety by training practitioners to ignore or accept with detachment loud noises and other disturbances that might otherwise create greater anxiety (Scott, 2021).

Another benefit is great emotional resilience and stability. The art of observing trains your brain to acknowledge your feelings and let them flow by without getting stuck in them.

Focus meditation trains you to stay in the moment, to be present and aware of what is directly in front of you. It can give you the confidence to deal with present issues without distractions and emotional baggage.

What Can I Focus on?

You may choose almost any object or subject that appeals to you. This can be a material object such as a feather or a flame, a physical sensation like the rise and fall of your breathing; or an abstract such as a visualization.

A sound or a chant is one of the most popular subjects for this type of practice. Some may choose a mantra or an affirmation, others a singing bowl, chimes, or other sound or music.

A candle flame, smoke from an incense stick, or reflections of light can be other subjects to try.

Nature offers unlimited potential subjects, too. From flowers to rocks, to tree bark, to shells and stars. Whatever calls to you will be the best subject for you at that time.

Try This: Calling in a Specific Angel Through Focused Meditation

This meditation can be used to call in a specific angel by name or to call in angels for protection, healing, and to problem-solve at any time.

If you have an angel you'd like to call in at this time, you can use this meditation as a template by substituting their name. For those who don't have a particular angel in mind, we'll call in Archangel Raphael—the Angel of Healing.

To focus on Archangel Raphael, we can use an icon or image. Raphael's color is purple and his plant is lavender. Concentrating on one or the other will work just as well, as well the scent of lavender essential oil or fragrances. Alternatively, if none of the above appeals to you, write down the Archangel's name on a piece of paper and use that visual as your focus.

You can also use visualization to picture your understanding or experience of Archangel Raphael in your mind. You can also use an amethyst crystal or chant the angel's name. All that matters is that you have a focus for the meditation.

Allow 10 to 15 minutes for this mediation, less (but not less than seven minutes) if you're doing this for the first time or you are currently short of time.

If you wish, you may now think of a question for the Archangel of Healing, or you may remain open to any messages or healings he may have for you.

Focus Meditation to Call in An Angel: Archangel Raphael for Healing

Are you sitting or lying comfortably? Ensure, if you're focusing on an object that it is within your sight. If it is a scent that you can smell well, or a sound that you can hear clearly. If you are ready, we'll begin by setting our sacred circle quickly.

Take a deep cleansing breath and see with your mind's eye the golden laser pen appear. Draw your circle of light, filling in the space with the highest frequencies of light and love, making it so that all dense and negative energies within and without are transmuted into the highest frequencies of joy and well-being.

Once your circle is up and you feel safe, it's time to focus on the subject representing Archangel Raphael.

Breathe in and notice the lines and contours you see. Breathe out and notice even more. Notice the color—the purple or the lavender. Allow yourself to move deeper into the color. Surround yourself with the color. Draw it around like a comfortable blanket.

Note the features of Archangel Raphael. Chant his name in your mind and concentrate on it. All your attention is on the sound, the color, or his features. When you lose track of time and are only aware of Raphael, keep doing what you're doing. Soon, you'll see Archangel Raphael appear in your mind's eye.

Thank the Archangel for his presence. Discuss your health issue with him and request his help with healing, or ask him if he has a message for you.

Drink in the color and scents of Archangel Raphael, or allow yourself to zone out as he gently works a healing on you. If he has a message for you, listen intently, hear the vibrations of his voice—real or imagined—and feel your vibration raise with his help.

If you have time, you may ask Archangel Raphael for more health advice. When you're done, it's time to thank Archangel Raphael. You may give him a hug (energetically, of course!) if you so wish.

Become aware of the lines and contours of your original focus. Feel the lavender and purple colors stir more healing next to you.

State that this healing will be active and integrated into your experience immediately with grace and understanding.

If you still feel Archangel Raphael around, ask if there is any other message for you. If there are none, thank Archange Raphael once more and see him fade into the image or object you originally focused on. Notice the color, the smell, and the contours of that object.

Slowly, become aware of the world around you. Blink, refocus your eyes, and move your fingers and your feet. Wiggle your toes and fingers.

See, in your mind's eye, the circle of golden light. With the pen of pink light of love, trace over the golden circle, transforming it into a pink circle of love. Infuse this circle with Raphael's purple light of healing. When you're ready, see the pink and purple circle dissolve into the world and the universe.

When you're ready, open your eyes if they've been shut. Stretch, yawn, and know that you can call on Raphael, anytime again.

If you are having a dry creative spell, you can try a similar Focus meditation with Archangel Gabriel. For help with healing love and friendships or finding new relationships, you can try a similar meditation with Archangel Chamuel.

Chapter 4:

Move in a New Direction

Did you know it's possible to multitask even more with meditation? Movement meditation is a great way to combine your daily exercise routine and develop your meditating muscles. If you have trouble sitting still, this is the meditation technique for you to begin with.

What is Movement Meditation?

Movement meditation is the combining of mindfulness with slow, gentle, flowing movements that are repeated. Some people prefer a faster pace and may meditate when jogging or running. You'll hear marathon runners speaking about getting into the zone which is essentially a meditative state. The important thing about movement meditation is that the actions are repetitive and that your concentration is mostly on your breathing and the performing of the action.

While moving, your attention alternates between focus and open awareness of your body, its movement, your environment, your thoughts, and any insights you may have. It sounds like a lot to do at once, but it's fairly simple to begin with.

Types of Movement Meditation

A movement meditation can be applied to almost any action including housework (mopping and sweeping) and even knitting and sewing.

This meditation technique is most often applied to walking, dancing, yoga and pilates, Qigong, Tai Chi, and other martial arts. For those with mobility issues, movement meditation can be adapted to individual circumstances.

Walking meditations can be easily done by most mobile people with no extra cost and little additional effort. Dancing can integrate awareness of the music and your body's responses to it. Yoga and pilates are great for breath awareness and mindfulness while holding stretchings and concentrating on holding the positions.

Qigong and Tai Chi both also focus on the movement of *chi* or energy through your body and also incorporate some visualization. Although they may take some time to perfect, they often show quick, noticeable results to your overall well-being.

Tips of Movement Meditation

Before beginning the meditation:

- Wear comfortable loose clothing and shoes. Chafing and pinching can draw you out of your meditative mindset.

- Choose a space that allows you sufficient freedom of movement for your movements. You'll want to stretch or swing to full arm's length at least, and for walking or jogging meditations, you'll need either a safe circuit (even if it's only up and down your street), a park, or an official trail. As you will be focusing on your breathing, you may also want to consider air quality, too. Natural and calm surroundings are best, if available.

- Decide if you'd like to use music as an accompaniment or, if outdoors, the sounds of nature and your immediate environment will serve instead.

During the meditation:

- Be aware of your inhales and exhales. Do your best to synchronize them with an action. Spending the first two or three minutes on establishing this synchronization is often worth the effort as it soon becomes automatic and your attention can be turned to other aspects that you may consider less often.

- Use slow deliberate movements. If you're doing two different motions simultaneously, you may want to first give your attention to the one action, then blend in the other action for better results. This will allow you to watch how you integrate and adapt to new or complicated situations.

- Listen and observe your body and its journey through the world. You may feel muscle groups you have never been aware of before and realize where and how you hold stress in your body. The mechanics of your body may surprise you.

- Notice your environment. The swish of air over your arms and legs, the change of surface moving from grass to gravel, the volume of a sound varying as you go around corners. Notice everything and be in the moment.

- If thoughts of work or worries intrude, acknowledge them and set a later time to consider them, then return to your body, your movement, your environment, and your passage through it.

- If you find your creative juices flowing, make a mental note to follow up on that idea and continue with your focused attention on your movement.

- Acknowledge your progress at the end of the meditation. It's confirmation of your self-growth.

- If you're doing prescribed formal movements such as Tai Chi, remember that all your practice movements should be mindful, too.

Try this: Movement Meditation and Healing from the Angels

Angels make great walking companions, especially when you're off by yourself! Not only can they help you problem-solve while walking, but they can help you heal by working through emotional upsets or physical pain.

For this meditation, you'll need a safe, or well-known space to walk in for about 15 to 20 minutes. This can be your walk to work if you don't have dangerous crossings or similar hazards to navigate. If that is the case, you can do a regular walking meditation by paying particular attention to your breathing and your environment.

Your backyard or balcony can also be used if it is large enough for you to swing your arms and take a few strides. You can also do this meditation on a treadmill or a stationary exercise bike if you so wish and have them available.

Be sure to carry some water for hydration or have it handy, especially if it's a hot day.

Go through the tips for moving meditations, choose your route in decent weather if you're heading outdoors, and when you have all that you need, we'll begin.

A Walking Meditation With Angel Healing

Have you got everything you need? Are you comfortable and ready to begin? Take a moment to ensure you are organized for your walk (and your keys are put away, if need be).

Let's start with a big breath. Swing your arms in an arc and let them fall loosely. Repeat the arm motion and as you do imagine a protective bubble of golden light slightly bigger than the arc of your arms cocooning you in safety and filtering out all negativity. Loosen your shoulders and stretch your legs. Feel your muscles contract and relax and be aware of the air temperature. Stretch again, if you'd like, noticing where you feel loose and tight. When you're ready. Take the first steps on the route you've chosen.

Take a deep breath. Feel your chest contract and relax. Hear your breath and become aware of your heartbeat. Do this as many times as you'd like. When you feel comfortable and in this rhythm, we'll open our hearts, clear our energy and invite our angels (or a particular angel if you'd prefer) to accompany us on this meditation.

Now that you're ready to open your heart, take a deep breath and know that your heart is blossoming, glowing stronger and stronger, your heartlight cheerfully washing through your body from the top of your head to the tips of your fingers and toes. Repeat this until you're smiling or feeling lighter-hearted. Notice the power in your legs pedaling you forward and the feel of the surface beneath your shoes. Notice the swish of air as you swing your arms freely, and how easy and free your movements are.

Turn your attention inwards and to your crown—the space about a palm's length above the top of your head. If it is a sunny day, feel the sunshine beam down on you carrying the golden light from Source bathing you in cleansing light infused with every frequency. If you are indoors, visualize the sunshine beaming down on top of your head and feel the warmth surrounding you and cleansing you in the same way.

In your mind's eye, see the golden light washing over every cell in your body, every aspect of your being, and through all your energy fields, washing away all negativity, all energetic debris, and any blockages since your last cleansing. See this light moving down your legs and into the earth, tethering you to the heart of Gaia. There, all negativity is transmuted into love, light, and nourishment, and is returned to you via your tether, its sparkling energy zinging up your spine and out through the top of your head to Source, forming an equal exchange of beautiful energy.

Turn your attention to your environment. Notice the sky, the plants, the colors, the smells, the textures. If any other thoughts intrude, know that you will deal with those issues later. For now, you are enjoying the movement of your body and the space around you.

It's time to call upon your angels. Invite your highest frequency angels to walk with you for a little while. Ask for a sign that they are with you, if you so wish. Become aware of your angel beside you. If you like and have not called them by name, you may now ask for it. If you like, you can also ask them to verify themselves to you with your sign from your first angel meditation. This isn't necessary if you are already familiar with the presence of your angels.

As you walk, tell your angels of your emotional upsets or other issues that are bothering you or stressing you out. Ask for their advice. You may find that this turns into a counseling session with your environment underlining some messages from your angel, like a signpost echoing your angel's words.

If you're experiencing pain or a physical ailment, ask your angel for advice in managing it. Ask your angel if it is possible to relieve your pain with every step you take to your destination. If the answer is yes, then notice the area of pain and discomfort and the diminishing of that painful sensation. If the answer is no, ask for more solutions to help manage your situation.

When the conversation with your angel and the healing is at an end, thank your angel, and if you'd prefer, ask them to continue accompanying you.

Turn your attention back to your body. Notice any differences in your movement, your body, or your outlook since you began the meditation. Notice your environment, the play of light, the sounds, and the activity.

Take a deep breath and feel the rise and fall of your chest. Hear your heartbeat. Feel the power and miracle that is your body.

Continue your mindful awareness until you reach your destination. End with a deep breath and some stretching. Send gratitude to the angels, to Gaia, and to your body. Enjoy the miracles all around you.

If you enjoy this meditation, it goes well with the Loving-Kindness Meditation. Try *adapting this meditation to stationary cycling, yoga, and Qigong. It can also be done on a ferry or bus ride.*

Chapter 5:

Discover Your Mantra

A mantra is a word or phrase that can empower you. Through sound and resonance, mantras can change your mindset and elevate your health. Similar to, or even incorporating affirmations, mantras can be as simple as a repeated sound or a multi-concept statement of your reality. For example, a simple sound would be 'Om' or 'Aum' that's said to resonate with the creation of the universe.

A multi-concept statement may be something along the lines of: I easily find all I need to experience joy and well-being whenever I choose to. This statement is affirming that experiences of joy and well-being are always available to you, but you are giving yourself the option to experience other emotions in life as well. This mantra also affirms your power over your life and your emotions, and if you are not experiencing joy and well-being, it is providing you space to make choices that will bring them in with ease.

What is Mantra Meditation?

Mantra meditation is a form of Focus Meditation. Your focus will be on your vocalization, and the intention behind it. Sometimes, the mantra may be a statement that is designed for reflection, opening the door to an awareness meditation. Often mantras are chanted. Some prefer to regulate their breathing with each recitation of the mantra.

Meditating with a mantra can benefit you in the same ways as other meditations. It's particularly good at reducing stress and anxiety, generating calm, and boosting self-esteem (Dibenedetto, 2016)

(Raypole & Legg, 2020). An additional benefit is of it potentially realigning the way you think and respond along more positive and less reactive lines.

In other words, mantra meditation can help overcome habits and alleviate certain psychological conditions by forging new, beneficial links in your brain. In essence, given time and persistence, it can reboot and upgrade aspects of your thinking and functioning.

Chanting a mantra out loud can help improve your memory and enhance your learning abilities by synchronizing your left and right brain (Raypole & Legg, 2020).

Mantra meditations needn't be long to be effective. Much like Focus Meditation, a few minutes a day can quickly calm you and shift your mood and concentration to higher levels.

Can I Make my Own Mantra?

Yes, you can! This is a wonderful way to adapt your meditations to your current situation. Crafting your own affirmations is also a great way to use this meditation technique if prescribed chants and mantras (particularly if they aren't in your native language) don't appeal to you.

Before you decide on your mantra and affirmation, it would be good to try different ones to find what feels and sounds good for you. This will also help you tailor your personal mantras and meditations.

Create Your Own Mantras and Affirmations

As your situations change, so will your mantras change. Consider experimenting with sounds, words, word order, and length. Say them in your mind, and say them out loud. Much like trying out clothes while shopping, try out your mantras and affirmations until you find the ones that fit your current situation best.

To create your own affirmation or mantra follow these steps:

1. Pick a word that describes the solution to the issue you'd like to work on or contemplate. For instance, if you're feeling anxious, your solution may be *ease* or *safety*, or *joy*. If you have more than one language or a translation of the word appeals to you, add it to your solution. For example, if your solution is love, you may want to add *amor*; if it's joy, you may want to add *alegría*. Take your time and find a list of words to play with for the best effect.

2. Experiment by saying this word out loud or under your breath. How does it feel? If it feels right, continue to experiment with finding a rhythm in repeating the word. Voicing the word on your exhale is a sure way to find your natural rhythm. If you like singing, try singing out the word. When you find a method that feels and sounds good to you, you have your mantra!

3. Expand your one-word mantra into an affirmation by constructing a sentence that conveys your ideal self or situation. One of the simplest and most powerful ways to achieve this is by adding the phrase "I am." Your affirmation for love can then be "I am Love." Your affirmation for joy will be "I am joy." Don't be afraid to combine complementary elements into one affirmation. So, the two preceding examples can be harmoniously combined into "I am love. I am joy," or "I am love and joy."

4. It's best to keep your mantric affirmations simple, but if you wish, you can expand them further or modify them to address certain issues specifically. Here, you may wish to use "I have," or "I experience." To alleviate anxiety, you may try something along the lines of "I have strength. I have support," or "I experience ease and safety wherever I go."

5. Keep experimenting and refining your affirmation or mantra. Add to the front, edit out the middle, rearrange and find the right meaning, intention, and rhythm for you. If you're wishing to alleviate pain or another chronic issue, you may want to try

even more specific affirmations. You can modify "I am comfortable and at ease in my body" to "With each breath I take, I reaffirm the strength, resilience, and comfort I experience in my body. With each breath I take, I grow stronger, healthier, constantly healing all hurts until they are fully healed."

Tips on Chanting Your Mantras

- If you feel too self-conscious about chanting or speaking out loud, whisper the mantra or say it under your breath.

- Use the breath on your exhale to resonate the words through your body and energy field.

- Try varying your speed of voicing the words or dragging out certain syllables until you feel your body respond to the mantra and frequency. That is the ideal speed for you at that time.

- If you have two words, try repeating the shorter word twice to every one of the longer words, for example: joy, joy, *alegría*.

- Change the rhythm or speed if you find your attention wandering.

- Keep some water close to hand, and hydrate before you start chanting.

- If you'd like to count off your repetitions and don't have mala beads, listen to the ticking of a clock, or set an instrumental track to accompany you. Ensure the sound is softer than your voice as your awareness needs to be on the mantra and not the background sound.

What are Mala Beads and Do I Need Them?

Mala beads are a circle of 108 beads plus an extra bead called the 'guru' bead. Used extensively in the eastern traditions, its western equivalent would be rosary beads. During mantra meditations, they're used to count off 108 repetitions of a mantra, an auspicious and mystical number from the Hindu tradition that often uses mantras as prescribed remedies for certain problems.

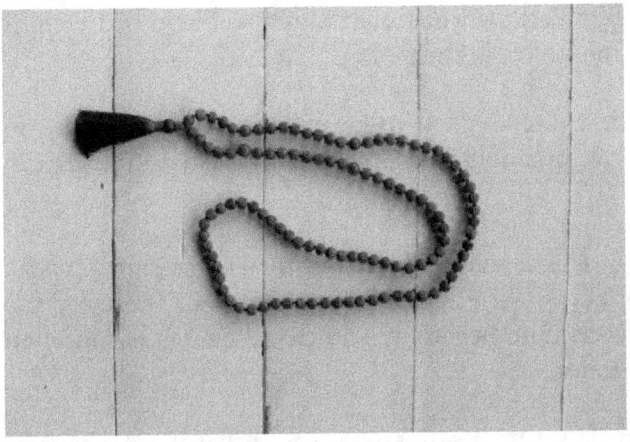

The action of counting off the repetitions—one bead per repetition—is believed to help you concentrate on the meditation.

Using mala beads isn't necessary for practicing mantras and affirmations. They're an additional accessory that may be helpful, but could also be a hindrance, depending on your preferences. Give them a try if you're curious but know that all you truly need to practice mantra meditation is some time, your mantra, and a comfortable place to sit.

Try This: Angel Protection/Healing and Mantras for Times of Extreme Anxiety

When the world gets a little too crazy and circumstances outside our control threaten our peace of mind and sense of security, help from our angels is always welcome.

This meditation calls on angels of protection and angels of healing to work together to ease situations while our mantra will help address our anxiety while aiding the angels in their work.

Remember to take deep breaths and to keep things simple. Once you find your calm and the situation eases, more complicated mantras can be done.

If you have a rose quartz crystal or black tourmaline or onyx crystal, feel free to hold it or keep it close by while you meditate. These crystals will help calm and transmute negativity and dense energy around you while elevating your mood.

In this meditation, we'll set up a safe sacred space that the Archangels will oversee. We'll invite angels of healing and those specific to the situation, if need be. While the angels hold the space and conduct their healing, we'll craft a mantra or repeat one we already have until our anxiety eases. Once the healing is felt or our anxiety eases, we'll thank the angels and close the meditation.

You can do this meditation in any space, including on public transport and airplanes, and even while standing in line in places you feel unsafe. You can add elements of this meditation and healing to your walking and jogging meditations if you feel called to.

Angel Protection and Healing Meditation with Mantras for Times of Extreme Anxiety

Feel your feet planted firmly on the earth, supporting you. Take a deep breath, and release it slowly, almost like a sigh. Feel your shoulders ease and your chest open up. Take another deep breath and notice again how firmly you sit in this world. Imagine a line from the soles of your feet stretching down into the heart of Gaia, anchoring you to all the love and support in the world.

Take a deep breath and feel the love flowing up these lines filling you with love from your feet all the way up to the tip of your head and flowing upward along the extending line to the heart of Source. Take another deep breath and feel the love returning along the line from Source, filling you and passing on down to Gaia.

Notice that you are calmer and think clearer now. When you're ready, we'll call on the Archangels and secure the space around us. When we call on the Archangels, see them each take position by your shoulders and to your back and your front so you'll be in a square or circle guarded by them. It doesn't matter if you can't imagine what the angels look like. Just know that they are there.

Now, say these words in your mind or similar words to the same effect:

> *I call on Archangel Michael and the angels of protection to keep me and mine safe and protected from all ills, violence, and negativity.*
>
> *I call on Archangel Gabriel and the angels of communication to keep my messages clear and understood so there can be no more misunderstandings, and so that I can be heard.*
>
> *I call on Archangel Uriel and the angels of technology and unseen mechanisms to keep all systems and technologies available and in good order to ensure this situation is resolved with ease and grace.*
>
> *I call on Archangel Raphael and the angels of healing to help heal this situation in all ways for everyone concerned.*

> *I ask for the Archangels' help for as long as it is needed.*

See the angelic forms glow in your mind's eye. Feel their presence and reassurance. Know that no matter how scared you may feel, the angels will protect and assist you in the best ways possible and for your best outcome.

Take a deep breath and feel how much calmer and more collected you are. Prepare to call in the angels of healing specific to the situation. If you are anxious about someone in your presence or afraid for dear ones in a similar situation you can include them in the situation, but know that the angels can only intervene where they have permission to.

Let's invite the angels of healing now.

Say these words or ones to similar effect:

> *I invite into this space the highest frequency angels of healing and angels (specific to this situation) to help heal and reconcile this situation. I remain open to their signs and guidance and ask that it be made known to me when the situation is sufficiently healed and reconciled so I may be reassured. I trust in the healing and reconciling process that is now underway and thank the angels for their help.*

If you are feeling sufficiently calm, you may close the meditation here. If you are still feeling anxious or would prefer to meditate further, we'll work on your mantra.

In your mind's eye, see the angels all around you, healing the situation, protecting you, and bringing ease and grace to everyone. Notice your feet firmly grounded on the floor, still conducting love up and down you and all the way to Gaia's heart and the heart of Source. Feel this glow of love.

In your mind say these words or ones to the same effect:

> *I am protected. I am safe. Love is all around me now. It strengthens me and is reflected back to me.*

Repeat the mantra as many times as you wish and for as long as you wish. If you are on a long journey and fall asleep, that's okay. The angels will continue to hold your space and run through the healing process for as long as you need.

When you are ready, calm, and satisfied the situation is healed or stabilized in positivity, it's time to thank the angels.

You may say the following or similar:

I thank the angels of healing for their help, their healing, and their love. I send love to them.

I thank Archangel Michael and the angels of safety and security for their protection and guidance.

I thank Archangel Gabriel and the angels of communication for their help and support.

I thank Archangel Uriel and the angels of technology and the unseen for their help and support.

I thank Archangel Raphael and the angels of healing for their presence, healing, and support.

I send all the angels love.

I send all those present, and affected by the situation, love.

You may feel this love returned to you as warmth or a feeling of being hugged. Know that you are loved and protected and that your well-being matters to the angels and those around you. Send out gratitude if you so wish, and then it will be time to close the meditation.

Feel how firmly your soles sit on the ground, anchoring you in love to the constant flow of light and love from Gaia and Source. Know that you are a part of this love and you carry it always with you.

Take a deep breath, and let it out slowly, almost like a sigh. In your mind say something to the effect of:

I thank the angels and Archangels for holding this safe space for me and mine for as long as it is needed. I send all my love.

If your eyes were closed, you may now open them. Stretch if you can, wiggle your toes and shift your shoulders. It's time to continue with your day.

If you find yourself stuck in a difficult situation or are in a neighborhood that you no longer feel safe in, you may do this meditation, or modify it, for daily use. You can invite others in your family or community to join you if you so wish.

Chapter 6:

Time to Consider Transcendence

Transcendence. Does the sound of if immediately bring to mind saffron-robed mystics sitting on mountaintops for years on end to attain Nirvana or bliss? While the popular perception is that transcendence is a mystical, almost unattainable pursuit, there are ways for you to achieve it without ever leaving town, albeit with some special guidance and a lot of perseverance. Transcendental Meditation, also known as TM and the only trademarked meditation, is the next popular meditation technique to consider.

What is Transcendental Meditation?

TM is a prescribed form combining mantra and spiritual aspects of meditation and is primarily based on traditional Vedic (Hindu) meditation practice. It seeks to move an individual through various states of consciousness until they reach Unity Consciousness. There is some debate as to what degree it is a religious meditation. Practitioners meditate for 15–20 minutes twice daily after undergoing formal training in the seven-step process. The cost of training in this form of meditation varies based on your location.

Due to its earlier popularity, more research has been done on TM than on other meditation practices.

A Brief History of Transcendental Meditation

In 1955, Maharishi Mahesh Yogi began widely teaching Transcendental Deep Meditation based on his learnings from Brahmananda Saraswati. The meditation technique was renamed Transcendental Meditation.

After 1958, the meditation became popular in the West after endorsements by celebrities and research that indicated its benefits of stress reduction and greater relaxation, better heart health, and greater self-awareness (Wikipedia, 2022).

The multinational Transcendental Movement grew tremendously into the 2000s and it's estimated that millions of people have trained in this meditative form. Today, schools and universities have grown up around the movement and associated programs are now run at various institutions globally.

Controversies

Although there have been many research papers confirming the claims of TM, most of these studies were believed to be subjective as the researchers or funding had links to TM practitioners. TM's branches of Science of Creative Intelligence and the Maharishi Effect have not been confirmed as holding true scientific concepts and have been labeled pseudoscience by many scientists.

The Transcendental Movement has also been accused of being cult-like in its methods and structure by some, and just a repackaging of traditional Hindu beliefs and practices by others.

Some individuals have reported adverse effects on mental health when practicing TM. Care must be taken if you have a known mental health issue when practicing TM (Ansorge & Wheeler, 2022).

Whatever your view of TM, its outstanding contribution to self-help and meditation fields is to make something that looks and feels mystical and difficult attainable to anyone who is interested in trying it out.

Does it Work?

As with Mindfulness and Spiritual Meditation, Transcendental Meditation may help alleviate pain, depression, and anxiety. The American Heart Association considered TM as a likely complementary treatment for hypertension, while the *Psychological Bulletin*, journal found some data that suggest an improvement in learning and memory, a more positive outlook, reduced anxiety and neuroticism, as well as great self-actualization when practicing TM (Wikipedia, 2022).

Since the late 1970s, Transcendental Meditation and its related fields have been offered widely across institutions including schools and prisons in the Americas, India, and Europe—to some controversial effect as the debate as to its religious and cultish nature continues.

How Do I Learn Transcendental Meditation?

The best and only way to learn TM is through a Certified TM teacher through a Transcendental Meditation organization in your area. Your training is most often a seven-day process tailored specifically to you.

What to Expect During Your Transcendental Meditation Course

The process has seven steps that your teacher will lead you through. Once you complete the steps and are initiated, you can practice TM by yourself.

After receiving two lectures (an introductory and a more in-depth one), you'll be interviewed by your teacher for a few minutes. Thereafter you'll receive instructions over a one to two-hour session. The next meeting with your teacher will include an initiation ceremony where you'll be bestowed a personal mantra or sound.

Over the next three days, you should receive another one to two-hour session each day to correct your technique, answer questions, and provide more information as needed. After this session, you can practice alone, checking in with your teacher occasionally whenever needed or for follow-ups.

Chapter 7:

Progress a Little Further

If pain management or muscle tension from excessive stress is a major concern of yours, a Progressive Meditation Relaxation (PMR) could help. Add in a Body Scan to find those deeply held in tissue emotional issues and you have multi-faceted meditation to address your concerns.

What is Progressive Meditation?

Ever repeatedly squeezed your fist shut, then released it. That is basically what progressive meditation is. You release pain and physical tension by working through different muscle sets in your body simply by tensing, then releasing them.

Also called Jacobson's relaxation technique, this meditation type can alleviate migraines and their frequency, help with pain management, and promote better quality sleep. It has also been useful in anger and anxiety management. Research indicates this technique also positively influences our electro-physiological systems. Some prefer to do this meditation at bedtime to help them fall asleep as PMR also relaxes you mentally (Lui et al, 2020) (de Lorent et al, 2016) (Meyer et al, 2016).

How is a Body Scan Different?

Body Scanning is performed like a focus meditation, concentrating on a specific part of the body and noticing any sensations, discomfort, and feelings at that point. You may intuit a source of the sensations or discomfort, but you simply observe, acknowledge, and then move on to the next body part.

This technique also helps in de-stressing, alleviating pain, and profoundly relaxing the body so you can fall asleep.

It works well together with Progressive Meditation as the processes are so similar and the meditation can easily flow from one to the other.

What do I Need to Successfully do a Progressive Meditation?

To do a successful Progressive Meditation you don't need any special equipment. You do need some patience, a comfortable place to lie down, and time to work through the scan and progressive meditation phases.

Ensure that you won't be disturbed and that the time and place are quiet. Before you sleep or would like to take a nap is one of the best times for this meditation. Loosen any tight clothing and make sure you're in an area of good ventilation.

You are likely to stretch your limbs and shift your body weight from time to time, so it's best to make sure that you are able to stretch out fully for this meditation.

Try This: Body Scan and Progressive Meditation with the Angels to Help Heal Your Inner Child

Your Inner Child is that part of you that still carries the baggage from your childhood, often, in many of us, holding onto a myriad of hurts and beliefs that still greatly impact our current well-being. Healing your Inner Child can take a long time, so any little bit of understanding and healing of this aspect of yourself is a big step forward in your general healing and spiritual growth. An additional benefit of healing your Inner Child is that it can alleviate certain chronic conditions and stressors in your life.

Angels work well with your Inner Child. Besides helping you access your Inner Child, angels can also reassure and allow your Inner Child to feel safe, loved, and seen.

In this meditation, we are going to establish a safe space, then invite the angels and our Inner Child to reveal what needs to be healed at this time. Alternatively, you may choose a topic or incident yourself.

Once your Inner Child is accessible, we will run through the Body Scan with your Inner Child's help, then use progressive meditation to help release the issue where possible.

Remember to allow 20 to 30 minutes for the full scan. If you fall asleep during the meditation, that is okay. Continue from where you left off as soon as you can.

If you are concentrating on one part of your body and your attention suddenly switches to a sensation or pain in a totally different part of your body (for example, concentrating on your hand makes your neck hurt) then work on the part of your body to which your attention has been drawn (your neck in this example).

WARNING: If repressed memories and hurts are released, you may feel triggered by this meditation. Seek professional help,

journal your feelings and release the emotions. Allow yourself to cry and grieve if you feel the need. Find the support that you need and don't attempt this meditation again until you have healed that issue. Triggering emotions without addressing them isn't good for your mental health so ensure that you are prepared to immediately deal with any triggers you may experience.

Body Scan and Progressive Meditation with the Angels to Help Heal Your Inner Child

When you're lying down comfortably, we'll begin. Ensure you are warm and well hydrated.

Is your neck comfortable? Is your back straight? Can you breathe easily and naturally? If the answer is yes to all, then you are ready to begin. If not, take some time to make yourself comfortable. You will be lying down for a while.

When you are settled, take a deep breath. Hold for a count of two. Release slowly, expelling all the air out of your tummy. Repeat two more times, then breathe slowly and evenly.

In your mind's eye see a protective bubble of light form around you. Call on Archangels Michael, Uriel, Gabriel, and Raphael to guard over you. Make it so that the bubble of light is full of the highest frequencies of love, light, and healing. You see the bubble shifting into pink light from time to time. Know that you are safe and protected.

Into your bubble of light invite the angels of healing and your Inner Child. You may use these words or ones to the same effect:

> *I invite into this sacred safe space of light and healing the Angels of Healing and my Inner Child. I ask that during this meditation I receive their help in releasing and healing any and all issues that I am ready to let go of at this time. I also ask that I gently be made aware of any other issues I need to address soon and be given guidance on the best way to do so. I thank the angels and my Inner Child.*

Take a deep breath and release it. Notice how your chest and tummy tighten and release. Continue breathing easily. We will be tightening and releasing various sets of muscles as we go along. If you are unsure how to do it, you can tense that part of your body and then stretch. If you still are uncertain, let your imagination lead and see in your mind's eye that part of your body tense and then release.

We'll now start the process. If you have not already closed your eyes, close them now.

Relax your eyes. Relax your nose. Relax your forehead. Relax your mouth and your jaw. Take a breath and release it. Concentrate on your head: your eyes, your ears, your nose, your mouth, your chin. How do you feel? What sensations are apparent? Do you feel tension? Pain? Warmth? Cold? Discomfort? Or ease?

Notice the sensations. If there is any pain, ask the angels of healing to help you heal or alleviate the situation—whatever is best for you at this time. While the angels heal, invite your Inner Child to share any emotions or issues they may have at this time.

Breathe in and out with ease as your Inner Child reveals to you anything they would like to share at this time. They may speak to you or you may remember memories. Certain tastes and smells may return to you. Once your Inner Child has finished sharing, allow yourself to process the feelings and information. When you're ready, we'll begin the progressive relaxation to help us heal deeply.

Notice the top of your head. Is there any pain, any sensation? State that you release that pain or any discomfort with ease and grace.

Frown, then relax your forehead. Repeat.

Notice your eyes. Is there discomfort? Know that at any time you notice discomfort, your angels are working to release it into comfort and ease. Still, with eyes closed, squint or clench them shut further. Hold for a count of two, then release. Know that the issues your Inner Child brought up are being released and are fading, too.

Purse your lips and tense your nose muscles. Hold for a count of two and release. Repeat.

Tense your jaw. Release. Yawn. Repeat.

If you're feeling so relaxed that you feel you may fall asleep, wiggle your fingers and your toes until you feel more present. Let's continue.

Notice your neck and shoulders. Relax your jaw. Relax your neck. Relax your shoulders. Roll them if you feel the need. Are they tense? Do they hurt? Take a deep breath and ask your Inner Child if there is anything they'd like to share or have addressed now. Listen or observe the information shared. Allow yourself to process any emotions and memories whether they are good or bad. When you feel like continuing, take a deep breath.

Tense your jaw. Release. Tense and stretch your neck chin down, hold for two then release. Chin up, tense and stretch your neck. Hold for two and release. Hunch your shoulders, hold and release, knowing you are releasing any deep issues that your Inner Child is wanting to be healed at this time. Repeat the tensing of your shoulders and their release. Roll your shoulders and take a deep breath. Yawn if you feel the need.

If you're feeling like you may fall asleep now, wriggle your fingers and your toes. When you're ready, we'll go on.

Notice your chest, your tummy, and your spine. Relax your body. Breathe deeply and evenly. Notice any sensations and any pain. Do you feel tension or tightness anywhere? Is your tummy making a sound? Is your heartbeat discernable? Know that if you have any pain and discomfort, your angels are working to ease it.

Ask your Inner Child if they would like to share anything with you at this time. Take note of the information they share with you. Process through their message and let them know they are loved and heard.

When you're ready to release the issue, tuck in your tummy, then release. Breathe. Repeat twice more: tuck in your tummy then breathe. Notice the right and fall of your chest. Feel at ease.

Turn your attention to your hips, bottom, and thighs. Relax your hips, and shift them into a more comfortable position if needed. Relax your bottom and your thighs. Focus on your hips, your bottom, your thighs. Is there any pain, any discomfort, or any hot or cold sensations? Know that if anything needs healing, your angels are working on it.

Take a deep breath and with your attention still on your hips, your bottom, and your thighs, ask your Inner Child if they have a message for you or an issue they would like to bring to your attention. Note their messages and any issues. Give them a hug if you feel the need. Process the information, and when you are ready to proceed, take another deep breath.

Tense your hips and release. Then your bottom and your thighs: tense, release. Know you are releasing any old energies and emotions that you are ready to let go of at this time. Repeat the tense and release sequence with your hips, bottom, and thighs twice more. When you're done, wiggle your hips and shift your bottom into a more comfortable position. We are ready to move on.

Let's focus on your knees, your shins, and your calves. Give them careful attention. Is there any discomfort? Are they tense, painful, tingly? Do they feel stiff or a little numb? Relax your body as much as you can and continue noticing your knees to your calves.

Ask your Inner Child if there is anything they would like you to know now. If there is no message, move on to progressive relaxation. If there is a message, process it and let your Inner Child know they are loved and heard. Let them know that you will take action to move you both forward.

When you're ready to move on, take a deep breath. Holding your toes pointed, move them down, stretching your knee to the foot area. Hold, then release. Holding your toes pointing up, stretch your foot up and feel the release in your calf and shin muscles. Lift your knees, tense your legs and thighs, then release. Repeat. Let your legs lie loose. Shift your knees until they feel comfortable again. If your knees are still very stiff, you may want to massage them later.

We're almost done with the scan and progressive relaxation. We will work on your feet and arms and then end the meditation.

Notice your ankle and your feet. What sensations do you feel? Are they hot or cold? Do they feel cramped or sweaty? Are your ankles stiff? Take a deep breath and catalog all the emotions and sensations. If your attention is directed to another part of your body, allow yourself the space to attend to the other part, then return your attention to your feet and ankles.

Take a deep breath and ask your Inner Child if they have anything to share. When they are done or if they have nothing else for you at this time, let them know that you are there for them. Let your Inner Child know that you love them, you hear them, and that you will do what is best to heal them and your current self. Give your Inner Child a hug, and let them know you will never abandon them nor let them face the unknown alone.

When you're ready, breathe in deeply and exhale. Clench your toes, release. Repeat twice. Rotate your ankles first clockwise, then anti-clockwise. Repeat. If your feet still feel tense, point your toes up and stretch your entire foot and leg as we did before, then point your toes down and do the same.

Notice your arms and hands. How do they feel? Is there any tension or pain—any discomfort? How do your elbows and upper arms feel? Is there stiffness? Notice and acknowledge the information coming from your arms and hands.

Take a deep breath and release. Clench your fists. Release. Repeat three times. Rotate your wrists first clockwise, then anti-clockwise, repeating three times. Tuck your elbows close to your sides, then release. Repeat twice. Loosen your neck and shoulders. Then your elbows and hands again.

When you're done, relax your whole body. Breathe in deeply, filling your entire body. Release, feeling yourself sink into your bed or the ground. Tense your whole body. Release. Repeat. When you're done, take another deep, deep breath, filling up your whole body from the tips of your toes to the top of your head. Then expel all your breath, feeling yourself once again sink into the bed or ground.

Breath normally.

Thank the angels and your Inner Child with the following words or to the same effect:

> *I thank the angels of healing and my Inner Child for this healing and experience. I send them love.*
>
> *I thank the Archangels Michael, Uriel, Gabriel, and Raphael for their help, healing, and for holding this protected space for as long as I need. I thank them and send them love.*

Take another deep breath. Wriggle your toes, wriggle your hands, and yawn. Now, you may fall asleep if you wish.

If you would like to work with your Inner Child in other meditations, consider healing your Inner Child issues with a mantra meditation, a Loving-Kindness meditation, or a Visualization meditation in which you envision your happy, healthy Inner Child safe from harm and healed from traumas. Remember to call in the angels to help reassure and heal your Inner Child during these meditations.

Chapter 8:

Amplify The Good Vibes

We all appreciate kindness and compassion when they are extended to us, but seldom do we actively think of seeking it within ourselves and for ourselves. For those of us that need to counter our internal detractors and the aspects of the news that depresses us while making us feel, Loving Kindness Meditations (LKM) or Bhavana Metta (Metta) and Compassion Meditations offer a solution. Loving Kindness Meditation is also an excellent way to amplify the good vibes globally and within your relationships.

What is a Loving-Kindness and Compassion Meditations?

You may be familiar with Loving-Kindness meditation from "Sending Love" meditations, but if you're not, the concept and aim of this practice are very simple. With the help of mantras and visualization, this meditation amplifies feelings of goodwill and unconditional love for yourself, for others, and for the world or universe at large. With this meditation, you can go really big!

Compassion Meditation is similar to Loving-Kindness meditation, but where Loving-Kindness focuses on the positive emotions and good vibes, Compassion Meditation attempts to cultivate compassion and acceptance in an individual by having them imagine people in distressing circumstances and in need of help. This type of meditation may not be for all and can be distressing to individuals.

Both types of meditation originate from Buddhist practices. Today, the Loving-Kindness meditation has also been widely adopted or integrated in part by many courses on offer, and so does not always follow the prescribed Buddhist approach.

Does it Help Me, Too?

If you're wondering if practicing Loving-Kindness meditations only benefits others that you're focusing on, then your answer is no! This meditation benefits you, too! A growing body of research consistently confirms that Loving-Kindness Meditation grows self-love and self-compassion and alleviates feelings of depression and sadness, although studies don't yet agree to what degree (Zheng et al, 2015). Anecdotal evidence and consequent research further suggests that anyone from any culture and background benefits from Loving-Kindness meditation, helping individuals manage anxiety and post-traumatic stress, cope with dread diseases, improve specific mental illnesses, and positively improve personal interactions in society.

Plus you will gain the feel-good factor of knowing you are raising the kindness quotient around you as well as the regular general benefits of meditation such as reduced stress, better sleep, and so forth.

How To Do A Loving-Kindness Meditation

The Metta-based meditation usually lasts just over 25 minutes, taking you through five steps with each lasting about five minutes. You can choose to visualize people or light or to use mantras such as "May you be happy," or "May you be loved."

You will need a quiet space and free time when you will not be disturbed. Choose your mantra if you prefer not to visualize.

Ensure you're sitting or lying down comfortably. This meditation focuses on you, then on a friend or loved one, next on someone who you feel neither positive nor negative feelings toward, then on someone you are in discord with, and finally on all beings.

Begin by taking a breath and becoming aware of your body. Notice your breath and direct your thoughts and feelings toward happy feelings and well-being. If you're finding this hard to do, remember a happy moment without any attached story: receiving a compliment, finding the perfect gift, something that made your day. Allow that feeling to fill you. You may repeat your mantra if you prefer as you sit in this feeling of happiness and joy. If any negative or critical thoughts arise, gently redirect your thoughts to those happy moments.

After a few minutes of basking in this glow, think of a friend or a loved one. It can be a pet if you so wish. Feel your affection for them. Allow their affection and love to fill you. Now, send your love to them so there is a cycle of love being sent and received. Feel this cycle of love between you. Sit in this flow for a little while.

Next, choose someone toward whom you feel neutral: an acquaintance, the security guard outside the store, your friend of a friend, or an old colleague. Feel a warm glow of happiness and love. Send them this love and happiness and feel it returned.

Choose someone you're at odds with: a neighbor, someone on the council, a TV personality that always annoys you, and spend a few moments feeling your happiness and the love that surrounds you. There is more than enough for everyone. Now, send this person you're thinking of happiness and love. If you're finding it difficult, repeat the mantra "May they be happy." Feel the calm and peace within you and the flow of love. You may feel this happiness returned to you, or you may not. It does not matter. You are at peace and calm.

Finally, from your place of happiness and love, think of all living beings. If the concept is too big for you, just hold the intention that you're now focused on all beings. Send them all love and happiness or repeat your mantra. Do this for about five minutes.

When you're done, sit in your happiness and love for a minute or two more and feel all the love and kindness now circulating about.

When you're ready, blink your eyes if they've been closed. Take a deep breath and move your arms and legs slowly. You have now completed your meditation.

Try This: Loving-Kindness Meditation with the Earth Angels

In this meditation, we're going to call on the angels and guides to aid us in helping the earth heal where possible with love. It is excellent to do when areas have experienced great upheavals such as natural disasters or war. If you'd like, you can also use this meditation in a group to send love and healing to such areas or specific situations that are causing community or family upsets.

This meditation, or a shorter version, can also be added to a walking or kayaking meditation if you're out in nature, or to a Focus meditation if you'd like a longer meditation and to end on a high feel-good note.

We're going to follow the process of calling in the angels, then sending love to various aspects of nature and the universe we're in.

If you're ready, we'll begin.

Loving-Kindness Meditation to Help Heal the Earth and A Difficult Situation

Are you sitting or moving comfortably? Ensure you're warm and will be comfortable for a little while.

Take a deep breath and let it out with a sigh. Now, in your mind's eye see your angels walking or standing beside you. Your personal angels and the Archangels are present. If you cannot see them, it is okay. Know that they are there. You may feel or sense their presence in other ways. Thank your angels for standing with you.

State your intention to send love and healing out into the world. Ask the angels to help you and boost your signal of love and healing. Invite the angels of earth, air, water, and fire to join you, too. You may want to use the following words or something similar:

> *I ask the highest frequency angels to help me send love and healing through the universe. I invite the angels of earth, air, water, and fire to help me send love to their regions and healing where needed. I thank them and send them love. As I do this meditation, I know that I am safe and protected and have access to limitless love, always.*

Now that we have the angels present aiding us in every way, see your heart opening like a flower, a glow of pink light from it growing brighter and brighter. This is the infinite love in your heart. See it expand and engulf your body. The loving glow may expand to a hands-width from your body. Stretch it further if you wish.

When you're feeling warm and fuzzy or a little giggly, send love to every aspect of your being: from your head to your toe and everything in between, from your heart and into every cell in your being to the ends of your strand of hair, from your brain to your energy and nervous systems. Send love to your being and give yourself a hug if you wish.

Turn your attention to the angels of earth. See them hold your hand and stand with you, amplifying any and all love that you send to earth. From your heart, see a pink thread of beautiful love light flow into the heart of the earth. As your love reaches Gaia's love, you feel your love returned by Mother Earth. See your love flood the ground beneath you.

In your mind's eye, see your love and wishes for healing wash over all the earth, healing the landscape and converting negativity into positivity. See the plants and trees respond to this wave of love, sending you love in return. See the insects and other animals stop and send you back love, too. It is okay at this point if you can't seem to stop smiling. It is a natural reaction. Thank the earth and the earth angels and let the love continue flowing.

Now, see the angels of water stand beside you and allow them to take your hand to amplify the love you are sending out. See your heart send a thread of glowing love to the ocean, and another thread to the lakes, dams, and swamps. See waters glow pink or gold as your love and wishes for healing are acknowledged and felt. See the waters grow clear and healthy mirroring back your love and the marine and freshwater creatures send you love in return. Know that your love is helping them heal. Thank the angels of the waters and let the cycle of love flow.

Take a deep breath.

In your mind's eye, see the angels of air stand beside you. Allow them to hold your hand and to amplify the love and healing you are sending out. See your heart love glow brighter flowing out like a faint mist, rising all around you, wafting higher and higher into the air, filling up the sky like just after a beautiful sunset or at a new dawn. See your love permeate through all the places and spaces that air occupies, glowing for a moment with the love you are sending out. Feel the love returned, momentarily making you feel lighter.

See the birds and other flying creatures notice you and call a greeting if you're outside. Feel their love returned to you and know that you're helping them find safer homes and wonderful nutrients. Feel your love flow higher and higher into the atmosphere into the realm of the highest storm clouds and beyond. Feel the air in your face glowing pink with love, sending love to all the processes that make our weather systems, and know that your love is helping those systems stabilize and keep their natural cycles. Return to yourself and feel your heart glowing with the love you're sending out and love returned to you. Thank the angels of air and let the love flow.

Take a deep breath.

Feel the angels of fire around you; angels who regulate natural wildfires and put out malicious ones, who help infuse passion in beings, who help temper fire and burnouts wherever they may arise, and who help nurture new life with sparks of vitality. Feel their warm presence and allow them to hold your hand and amplify all the love and healing you are sending out.

See your heart glow brightly with unconditional love, with your highest wishes for healing for all. See your heart glow flicker like a flame and send out threads to all the organic and inorganic sources of fire and fuel for fire, and of all the wombs of new life and life that need a little more energy to heal. Feel your love and wishes of healing flow to all these places and spaces: to forests, grasses, and brush, to the sun, to all the seeds in the world, all the new life being birthed in that moment, to all the sick, tired and elderly to need just that little more energy to recover.

Feel your love and healing flow to them all. Feel their acknowledgment and the returning of their love and healing to you. Thank the angels of fire for their love and compassion. Let the love and healing flow.

Know that you, too, are always loved and healing when and where required.

See your heart glowing with love and well-being. Feel in your cells and the spaces between your cells. Know it permeates and heals all aspects of yourself. Know that it is infinite. Thank your physical body, and your consciousness for allowing you this experience of love. Give yourself a hug.

Take a deep breath. Thank all the angels and guides who assist you, all the people and beings in the world who share this planet and universe with you. Let the love flow and return as naturally as breathing.

Take a deep breath. Wriggle your fingers and toes, smile at someone or at nothing, and move your body.

In this meditation, we've concentrated only on Earth, Gaia and her beings, but you can adapt this meditation to any group of people, or any situation—animate or inanimate. Try adding your pets, your garden plants, and your local areas in need of love to bring it closer to home. Or, go all out and send your loving kindness out to the cosmos and everything in it!

Chapter 9:

Create Your New Visions

The power of your mind is one of your most amazing and potent life tools. By envisioning happiness and greater well-being, you can guide your mind into creating situations that bring in greater positive effects into your life. In short, if your imagination can conceive it, then your brain can figure out the steps to building it.

Visualization is also valued for its personal and professional goal-setting and achievement effects (Raypole & Legg, 2020) (Rollins, 2020). Professional athletes improve their performance by visualizing their wins and the success that follows. This not only works as a motivation tool, but it also alleviates or disperses any subconscious issues about attaining success while also providing various routes to that win.

What is Visualization?

When you were little, adults may have told you to stop imagining things. Now that you're older, you are given free rein to imagine all you wish—just as long as you call it visualization! Simply put, that is what visualization is—asking "what if?" and seeing the outcome in your mind's eye; imagining what it would look like and feel like to experience your ideal situation or place.

We have been using visualization in many of our meditations already when we've been seeing with our mind's eye. Generally, with just a little concentration, it is not difficult to imagine your happier self, your healthier self in a beautiful situation. In effect, when visualizing, we're creating a simulation of what we'd like to experience.

Guided visualization uses imagery, sound, and even recollection of senses and feelings. These visualizations are often used for healing, manifesting, and relaxation.

By allowing us to mentally 'practice' a situation, visualizating relieves anxiety, combats depression, and can even help with pain relief. Self-confidence is a great side effect of visualization exercises.

How Can I Use It in Meditation?

Visualization can be used during Focus and Body Scan Meditations or processing emotions. It can also be used in Mindful Meditations to see deeper into aspects and envision abstracts for better understanding and processing. Add it to a Mantra Meditation to visualize the positive effects of your Mantra on yourself and the people around you.

Visualization can also be used at the start of Focus Healing meditations to practice moving through difficult situations. For example, to help you overcome anxiety of being in big crowds after you've been in a small town or spent most of your time at home. It's also a useful tool to use before interviews and similar interactions.

Visualizing is also great for manifesting and stress management. On the one hand, imagining yourself reaching your goals, of meeting the love of your life, or moving with ease and free of pain is a way to align yourself with those goals and keep you positively focused on your next step. It can, therefore, also help you make better choices so you bring in or manifest those situations quickly and with greater ease.

On the other hand, visualization used for 'me-time' or 'time-out' from your work day or routine is wonderful for stress management. Imagining yourself on the beach in Hawaii during your 20-minute break may not give you a suntan, but it can give you the mental and emotional break to cope with continued work stress in a healthier way.

Visualizations are used extensively for healing and energy work. In the energy-clearing and loving-kindness meditation, we saw in our mind's eye how the energy and love flowed through us. Reiki and other energy workers will often close their eyes and visualize the energy they work with. Visualizing intangibles can make them easier for us to work with and through. Another example would be imagining love as a drawn cartoon heart balloon floating toward us.

Tips for Visualization

- Begin with grounding and simple meditation to get into the optimal state of visualizing.

- Use sound prompts or background music/ambient music to help you immerse yourself in the meditation more fully. Prepare these before you begin.

- Pause to fully imagine the image or to fully register the feeling during your visualization. This will have a greater effect than merely 'flipping' through images as you would a magazine. In other words, engage yourself as much as possible in the imagery.

- If you're having difficulty beginning a visualization:

  o Imagine yourself turning on a screen as if you're watching a video. See the images appear on the 'screen,' and 'zoom' or 'walk' into the image to visualize more powerfully.

  o Begin with a small detail. For example, if you're asked to visualize a door, see the handle first, then "zoom out" to the entire door until you're able to interact with the door by walking through it or opening/shutting it. If you are imagining a flower, maybe visualizing the stem first would also work better for you, then allow your inner gaze to travel up to the opening flower or to note the petals.

- There is no right or wrong image to visualize. It doesn't matter if your 'scene' isn't exactly like the guided visualizations or even if it isn't realistic. It's perfectly fine to imagine a purple sky or silver birds. It's your mind's interpretation of the symbols you're drawing on that matter—much like dreaming, except your conscious mind is driving it, not your subconscious.

If you are repeating a visualization, it's okay if there are differences in the 'scene' or even dialogue that you hear. Remember, visualization stimulates your mind to explore and discover new possibilities, so change is a good thing.

Try This: Visualizing a Path Forward with Angel Guidance

Often when we have multiple options—good or bad—and are at a loss as to which ones to take, we forget that we have angel helpers to aid us in determining the best way forward. This visualization will call on our guiding and personal angels to help us find our best path through multiple options or confusing choices.

You may want to decide on a problem you would like to solve or think deeply about options you currently face. If you feel you have no options, consider doing this visualization with the intention of discovering new options.

In this meditation, we'll call on the angels and explore three possible paths.

Allow about 30 to 40 minutes for this visualization. Ensure you are comfortable. Have water for after the meditation and a throw handy in case you feel cold during the meditation.

If you are using ambient music for this meditation, ensure the musical track is long enough, or set it to repeat so it loops through continuously.

You may lie down or sit during this meditation. When you're ready, we'll begin.

Visualization with Angel Help to Find the Best Path Forward

Take a deep breath and let it out with a sigh. Take another deep breath and slowly let it out, feeling your tummy and chest rise and fall. Take one more deep breath and hold it for a count of three. Slowly let it all out through your nostril. If you'd like, you may take a few more deep breaths in whichever way you feel most comfortable. If you have not yet closed your eyes, please close them now.

When you're ready to continue breathing slowly and evenly then turn your attention to your feet. Notice golden threads from your soles flow down for a few meters, then entwine to form one glowing cord. See that cord continue down into the sacred heart of Gaia, welcoming you. Feel yourself being nurtured and the reciprocal nature of your relationship to Earth.

Take a deep breath and imagine love and nutrients flowing up the cord, through your feet, your legs, your hips, your torso, your heart, your throat, your forehead, and through the top of your head. The cord winds its way all the way to the heart of Source. Feel the love from Source returned along the cord, through you, and into Gaia, starting the healthy cycle of love of Gaia, you, and Source.

Take a deep breath, filling yourself up with the love and golden light from Source and Gaia. Feel this light wash over you, cleansing your energy and energizing you. Bask in this light for as long as you wish.

It's time to call in the angels. First, we will get the Archangels to help us hold a safe space, then we will call on our personal and other relevant angels to help us with determining the best path for us at this time.

Take a deep breath and use these words, or ones of your choosing to the same effect:

> *I call on Archangel Michael, Archangel Gabriel, Archangel Uriel, and Archange Raphael to help me hold this sacred space of love and light of the highest frequencies. I also ask that these four Archangels help guide me toward the best choice for me at this time. I thank the Archangels and send them love.*

See the Archangels standing in a circle or at the corners around you. Greet them and ask them for any messages they may have for you at this time. When you're ready, we'll proceed.

We'll now call in our personal angels and helpers. If you have a personal angel, in particular, you'd like to call on, please add their name where appropriate. Say these words or ones to this effect:

> *I call on my personal angels to help me determine the best way forward at this time. I ask that their insight and knowledge be shared in such a way that I may accurately and easily understand the knowledge. I thank them and show them love.*

Notice your personal angels by your side. Know that they are ready to guide you as requested.

In your mind's eye, look straight ahead. A road or path looks straight ahead as far as the eye can see. When you're ready, take a step down this path, then another. You notice that you are covering ground rapidly, your angels beside you, the path unchanged, but the verges and scenery becoming more familiar. You are now at the "here and now." Just up ahead the path splits into three. You walk up to the junction and peer at each path. How do they make you feel? Do you have a preference? Can you see anything on them?

Let's consider the first path. Ask your angels what they can reveal about this path. Discuss with them your concerns about any information they just shared with you. Watch the path change as you discuss it. When the discussion is over, note how you now feel about this path. Is it more appealing? Do you think it is not the answer? Hold off on your final decision, there are two more options to explore.

Consider the second path. What does it look like? Is it more appealing than one? Does it look clearer than the first path? When you're ready, ask your angels about this second path. Note any warnings, any information about good fortune, and what the longer-term and shorter-term prospects on this path are likely to be? Discuss further your thoughts and feelings about this path and ask the angels to confirm what is true and what is not. Look carefully at this path again. Does it appear any different than before? Is it a better option than you thought? Hold off your decision. There is one more option to consider.

Consider the third path. Has it changed its appearance since you last saw it? How does it make you feel? Is it more inviting than the first and second paths? What are your questions about this path? Ask your angels what you should know about this third path. Discuss your concerns about any new information you've gathered. Feel free to compare longer and shorter-term most likely scenarios of the three.

When you're done, thank your angels and ask if they can help you overcome any obstacles on your chosen path.

When you are sure, announce your choice: the first, second, or third path.

Take a deep breath. Feel your angels around you. Those that are not allowed to help you journey further will remain behind and those that can still assist you will accompany you to help clear obstacles on this path.

When you're ready, thank the angels who remain behind and take your first step in moving forward, knowing that you do not walk alone unless you choose to. Your angels will be there even when not discernable.

As you step down your chosen path, take note of any changes that occur. Notice how you feel when you walk it. Notice what you like and don't like about it. Remember that you still have the power to change your mind and that this option will lead to other options.

When you've walked a bit more, you come to an obstacle. What is the nature of the obstacle? Can you move it, walk around it, climb it? If you can, do so. If you cannot, ask your angels for help and advice. Follow their advice or watch them remove the obstacle.

Now that the obstacle is gone, continue walking this path. Is it getting harder, easier, or neither? Take note of any signs and symbols. You may find them useful or waymarkers of your physical journey at a later stage.

You may reach another obstacle or several. Each time, see the obstacle being removed or overcome either by yourself or with your angels' help.

Now, you are at the end of the path. What does it look like? Is it beautiful and serene? Does it have anyone waiting for you? Does it lead to another path or possible paths? Take a good look around. How does your next destination feel? Are there things you wished you'd remember to bring with you? If so, make a mental note that you'll add them to your preparations for this path you've chosen.

If this path didn't work out for you, remember there are two others. Feel free to return the Here and Now with your angels' help and explore the other options.

When you've done exploring, return to the Here and Now. Thank the angels who've accompanied you. Send them love.

Remind yourself that you'll remember all relevant information, the obstacles you've met, and how to overcome them all.

Then, when you're ready, take a deep breath, noticing the rise and fall of your chest. Then take another.

Thank the Archangels for holding the space for you.

Wriggle your toes and your fingers, and when you're ready, you may rise and journal about this decision and your choice if you wish.

This exploratory journey meditation can be adapted to other self-exploration themes and needs, too. You could adapt this to explore ways to discover new career paths, to explore the best way for you to discover new love, or even which pet you should adopt next! You can also seek out different aspects of yourself through this method, remembering to ask the angels for their healing if you wish it to be a healing journey.

Chapter 10:

Connect to Your Higher Self

Higher Self can be a puzzling concept at times. It's a part of you that is often forgotten. Some like to think of it as your interface between this plane or dimension and others—your interpreter of the divine and spiritual realms. Others believe it is the divine aspect of your spirit self much as your fingers are an aspect of your hand. Still, others believe it is your angelic self. Most agree that your Higher Self is a high vibratory part of you somewhat like your soul, detached from your ego, and attached to your body energetically.

It is said to locate itself above your crown. Many believe your Higher Self is not subject to Time and therefore transcends it.

The concept of your Higher Self is not a new one. It can be found in most major religions (Wikipedia, 2022), although it has gained prominence since the New Age renewed interest in it and began actively working and connecting to it via channeling and meditation. Integration and communication with one's Higher Self have long been practiced by Asian religions such as Buddhism. It is believed that with union or integration with your Higher Self, you gain enlightenment, peace, acceptance, and vast cosmic knowledge.

Why Connect to My Higher Self?

Connecting to your Higher Self brings greater self-awareness and understanding by circumventing your ego. You are able to perceive experiences without distortion of your prior experiences and self-interest.

Integrating or operating from your Higher Self regularly raises your vibration. A higher vibration makes it easier for you to access feelings of happiness, joy, and unconditional love regularly or almost continuously. You often experience better health as well.

Regular communication with your Higher Self empowers you by allowing you to comprehend ideas that are beyond your conscious mind and ego's ability.

For those looking for more meaning in their life or feel a pull toward fulfilling a predestined path, your Higher Self acts as your guide on your "true path," and often corrects you when you wander off. Your Higher Self is also said to see the truth of things and can lead you to finding true answers.

On a more practical level, your Higher Self can often bring in information you don't have conscious access to. This may be a suddenly well-remembered remedy from your childhood that you can safely give to your child or take yourself if the pharmacy is closed. Or the route to a relative's house that you've only visited once before and in a different season. Some individuals can access past-life information and abilities after integration with their Higher Self.

Why Should I Have Angelic Protection When Speaking to My Higher Self?

Angelic protection during meditations and while speaking to your Higher Self prevents energetic interferences and distortion. Having angelic protection in place ensures that your space remains positive and your experience is one of a high vibration. It's easier to hold and maintain a strong connection to your Higher Self when your angels are around. Think of it as your angels providing a secure messaging service from Higher Self to you much as you'd send a person-to-person message on your phone.

Experiences with your Higher Self can unground you and take you quite deep into explorations. With angels present, you are often prompted to reground and held in a safe space until you regain all your senses. You can think of the angels as your meditation besties who always look out for you when meditating.

Try This: Conversation with Your Higher Self in a Safe Space

A conversation with your High Self is one of the best ways to accelerate your self-growth. It's also a good way to gain another perspective on your life, your achievements, and the belief systems you may have learned from others.

And, of course, your Higher Self also offers great insight into those big cosmic and Life questions you've been pondering.

In this guided imagery meditation, we're going to create a safe space, invite in the angels, then clear our energy. We'll then identify our Higher Self and have a conversation. So, have your questions ready.

Allow sufficient time for this meditation—at least a half hour or more as often people lose track of time during such sessions. Ensure you won't be disturbed during this meditation. It's not advisable to do this meditation before bed. Mid-morning to mid-afternoon on one of your days off would be best. This meditation works well as a group meditation where individual experiences will differ. Choosing to share your experiences, if in a group, can also help you process your experience.

You may sit or lie down for this meditation. You may grow cold during the process so please have a throw handy. If you are using candles or incense, please ensure they are safely contained and won't represent a fire hazard during this meditation.

Meditation for a Conversation With Your Higher Self in a Safe Space

When you're sitting or lying comfortably, bring your attention to your breath. Notice the rise and fall of your chest.

Take a deep, deep breath, all the way into your tummy. Hold for a count of two, then exhale, expelling all the air in your lungs and tummy. Hold for a count of one, then inhale deep, deep into your tummy again, noticing it change shape as you do so. Hold for a count of two then release as evenly as possible. Notice how your tummy changes shape. Take one more deep, deep, breath just as before. Release, then breathe normally. You should be feeling very, very relaxed. If you'd like, you can take a few more deep breaths, but be sure not to fall asleep!

If you have not closed your eyes, you may do so now.

When you're ready, see your heart open, blossoming like a glowing flower. The light from your heart is warm and fuzzy. It spreads through you and out beyond the widest stretch of your arms and feet. It cocoons you in a warm, fuzzy bubble of love. You may extend this bubble as far as you'd like.

Take a deep breath and let it out gently. It's now time to reinforce our safe space and call in the angels.

When you're ready you may say the following or something to the same effect:

> *I call on Archangel Michael, Archangel Gabriel, Archangel Uriel, and Archangel Raphael as well as the highest frequency angels of security and communication. I ask that they hold this space in the highest frequencies possible and fill this space with light and love, filtering out all and any negativity and dense energies. I thank them.*

See your bubble infused with gold and purple light. See the archangels around you, and know that the other angels you called are ensuring the space you're in is safe, secure, and in the highest vibration possible.

Now that our space is safe and filled with the healthiest vibrations, it's time to clear our energy.

Take a deep breath and let it out through your feet. See a golden cord extend from your soles to the center of Gaia. Along this cord, send Gaia love and healing. Feel this love returned to you three-fold, rising through the cord, through your feet, all the way up through your body, and extending out through your crown. Up and up this cord extends into the heart of Source. Feel yourself and Gaia connect to Source. Feel your combined love returned three-fold. Breathe in this love and know you are loved, safe and secure.

See a golden light from Source wash down on you, permeating your head, your brain, your sinuses. Filling all of your head, ears, and mouth. It cleanses, rejuvenates, and revitalizes you.

See this torrent of golden light washing down your throat and around your neck; rejuvenating, cleansing, and revitalizing.

The torrent continues down over your shoulders and down to your hands and into your fingers. Your arms and fingers tingle at the cleansing, the rejuvenating, and the revitalization.

Feel the golden light from Source wash down over your clavicle, over your torso, and through your heart and tummy. It cleanses, rejuvenates, and revitalizes your body.

The golden light continues down over and through your hips, your bottom, your thighs, your legs, your feet, and all the way down to the heart of Gaia. It continually cleanses, rejuvenates, and regenerates as it flows.

Take a deep breath and know that all impurities and lower densities are being transmuted in the golden light into the highest frequencies of love, light, and joy.

Feel the love and light return up from Gaia via your tethering cord and up to Source via your central column. You feel lighter, rejuvenated, and more relaxed than ever before.

Take a deep breath and release. We will now connect to our Higher Selves.

Turn your attention to the golden cord linking you to Source. Follow this cord up by climbing it, then further up.

You notice a bright light shining on the cord. What color is this light?

As you continue climbing the golden cord, you see the bright light resolve into a form. It looks like a person. What does this light being look like?

You reach the light being. It is smiling in welcome. You look around and see a faint pink bubble is all around you, the angels standing all along. It is your safe, protected space.

The light being invites you to sit, or maybe you stand. Both of you are comfortable. You may ask the light being its name. If it is not the same as yours, ask it why?

Study your Higher Self as you talk. Ask it any question you like. Note how it answers. It's voice, its tone. Is it humorous or serious? Light-hearted or very formal?

If you have a question you have always wondered about, you may ask it now.

Let the conversation go on for as long as it needs.

When you're ready to leave or your Higher Self indicates there is no more to say during this session, then thank your Higher Self. You may want to give it a hug or leave-take in whatever way feels natural to you.

When you're taking your leave, your Higher Self may remind you that it is always with you and may suggest another way to access it that may be more suited to you.

Become aware of your safe space again, the pink glow, and the angels standing all around. Locate the golden cord. When you're ready, slide down the cord easily and gracefully.

Feel yourself re-enter your body through your crown, your awareness linking your brain to your heart. Feel the warm glow of your heart and know you are still safe and all is secure.

Enjoy being in your heart for a minute or so.

When you're ready, notice your feet again. See and feel the cord that links you to the heart of Gaia. Send love to Gaia, and feel it returned to you as you sink your awareness fully into your body grounded deep into Gaia, like an astronaut slipping into a spacesuit.

Wriggle your toes and your fingers.

Take a deep breath. Then another. Thank all the angels and send them love.

When you're ready, open your eyes.

You may want to journal your experience. Drink lots of water and get a good night's sleep over the next few hours.

As this meditation is quite ungrounding, it's not a good idea to do it every day. If you must, you can do this meditation once a week, or every two weeks. The more you communicate with your Higher Self, the less deep you'll need to go in meditation to communicate with them.

As an alternative, try modifying this meditation and combining it with an Energy Clearing meditation or a Focus meditation. After the energy-clearing, before you thank the angels, you may want to try channeling your Higher Self by journaling your conversation with them. After our conversation, remember to reground thoroughly, thank the angels for holding the safe space and then do some exercise or other movement to ground even more.

Conclusion

Well done! You now are familiar with nine popular techniques for meditation. There are many more, but these should work to give you a comprehensive taster of meditations and how they work.

We hope you've tried out two or three of these techniques and are well on your way to finding which ones work best for you and which are best avoided for whatever reason.

We also hope you've found that 15 to 20 minutes daily or every second day to establish your meditation practice.

Don't give up on meditation if you find the first or second technique or session doesn't work for you. Meditation is like exercise—the more often you do it, the more your body and mind remember how to do it and the rewards.

Let's not forget why meditation is such a good use of those 15 to 20 minutes a day. Not only will it help you grow calmer, less stressed, more positive, and possibly enjoy better cardiovascular and mental health, but it also allows you time to refill your creative and spiritual cup. You will be more open to ideas, new experiences, and alternative solutions. In short, your enhanced mindset helps you draw on greater resources creatively.

If you're serious about starting a regular meditation practice, we'd like to share a Zen proverb with you:

> *You should sit in meditation for 20 minutes every day—unless you are too busy. Then you should sit for an hour.*

Keep In Mind

You are an individual. What works best for your friend or partner may not work for you. So, while you may feel going to meditation with a friend is less bothersome to you, it's a good idea to try a Mindfulness or Mantra Meditation by yourself. You're likely to be less distracted and more likely to see the whole meditation through.

If you feel you can't sit alone and still by yourself for five straight minutes, try setting a timer for three minutes and beginning a Mindfulness or Focus Meditation. You'll be surprised how quickly time goes by when you're focusing on something.

While you may be tempted to try the longer meditations first, it's often better to begin with the 5 to 10-minute meditations first and work your way into the longer, more intense meditations.

Hydration is vital. Meditating, especially with energy, can dehydrate your body. Reciting mantras is thirsty work. Have a refillable water bottle or a glass with a flask of water at hand. Coffee and tea are not recommended before, during, or just after meditations. Water is the best to bring your body back into balance and complete any cleansing effects.

Being comfortable for the entire duration of the meditation is vital. Don't underestimate the importance of temperature regulation. Not only does it keep you comfortable but it keeps you focused, too. Stopping halfway through a meditation to take off a sweater or to throw on a jacket breaks your flow and reduces the benefits. Good ventilation is equally important, particularly if you're burning candles or other scents. Open a window if possible. A good flow of air also prevents you from falling asleep before the end of the meditation.

You don't have to excel at, or even like, all the techniques or even the most common ones. Find one that works for you. There are many more meditation types and combination types that may appeal to you more. Don't be afraid to try movement meditations like Qigong and Tai Chi even though they may look a little intimidating or difficult to start with. Each one of those graceful practitioners was once an imperfect beginner, and chances are many of them still make little missteps and mistakes, too!

Meditation should be thought of as a habit. Habits take time to build and meditation can be substituted for another habit. Try turning off the news on TV and meditating instead. Or substitute a 10-minute meditation for a game on your phone. Or wake up 15 minutes earlier in summer and give a morning Loving-Kindness meditation a try for a great start to your day.

Meditation has no shortcuts. The most effective ones train your brain and body to produce long-term and sustained benefits to your body, mind, and spirit. Keep in mind your true goal and you will be more motivated to stay engaged during meditation.

Remember, too, that as you change your preferences about meditation may change. Meditation can be adapted to all your life changes: from less time to lack of mobility, to changes in routine, and changes in environment. When you feel that something is no longer working for you, explore new options and adapt old ones. Take your focus meditation for a walk. Bring your loving-kindness meditation into your Progressive Meditation.

Additional Tips for Meditation

For visualizations and guided meditations, reading the words or script out loud generally works well in keeping you focused. However, if you have trouble visualizing images initially, you may want to record yourself reading the meditation out loud and playing it for the actual meditation. This also allows for a smoother meditation and one that you'll complete no matter the length because you are aware of the steps and are not likely to be distracted by wondering what comes next, or "will it be over soon?"

Don't feel bad about changing your mantras. Remember your mantras are a tool or prop to channel your focus and intention. When your focus and intention change, so too should your mantra. Otherwise, you'll be holding back your own progress.

For the most pleasant meditation sessions, eat a light meal a few hours before instead of a heavy one, and have a comfort break before you begin a session.

Tips for Hosting Group Meditations

If you enjoy a certain meditation technique and would like to share it with friends, family, or your community, you may want to keep some points in mind.

Before the meditation session

- Ensure the venue is large enough to host everyone and a friend if they bring someone along. This is especially important if you wish people to lie down on mats. Space people out as much as possible and allow their limbs to move freely should they have involuntary movements while deep in meditation.

- Ensure the venue is well ventilated and has climate control or something similar.

- Bring along extra covers and throws for additional warmth, even in summer.

- Carry water or make glasses and flasks of water available after the meditation. You may also want to remind participants to carry some along with a fruit, cookie, or even chocolate.

- The venue should be in quiet surroundings during the course of the meditation. Visiting the venue and planning ahead can avoid renovation or other environmental noise that will detract from the experience,

- If you don't own the venue, it may be better not to burn candles. If you're using incense, make sure it doesn't affect any other rooms and users of the venue.

- Sound is most important during the meditation. Participants need to hear every word said so they can safely and attentively follow along. Test the sound system and that it is compatible with your equipment before the meditation is scheduled to begin. Have a backup plan in case there's a problem. It's therefore always good to carry a printout of the meditation script or a book from which to read it out loud, or with a mic if the room is very large.

- Cleanse the room energetically before the meditation for the most positive experience for all. You can call in the Archangels Michael, Gabriel, Uriel, and Raphael to help you keep the room at a high, healing vibe.

During the meditation session

- Ensure everyone has gone for a comfort break and is settled before beginning the script of starting the audio.

- Try to remain calm and relaxed as you facilitate the meditation. Yelling or getting annoyed with people can be counterproductive and distracting for participants.

- It's important that if you are arranging and overseeing the meditation in a group that you don't close your eyes. Participants may need reassurance or your support during the meditation, and you having eye contact with them can be a great help. If any participants are experiencing unexpected reactions or fall asleep, you should monitor them.

- If there's a problem with the sound, immediately switch to your backup plan so no time is wasted and the meditation can easily continue from where it left off.

- Toward the end of the session, gently wake up anyone who may have fallen asleep. Don't call attention to them if possible.

- Let everyone ease out of their experience in their own time after they wiggle their toes and fingers.

After the meditation session

- Allow everyone to share their experiences if possible. Consider going outside or to a coffee shop if the venue is unavailable.
- Thank everyone for their presence and sharing.
- Clean up where necessary.
- Thank the angels for holding the safe space.
- Ensure you have your audio and books.
- Close any windows or doors you may have opened.
- Drink a lot of water, especially if you've been reading from a script.
- Have a shower.
- Do a short loving-kindness or mindfulness meditation for yourself.
- Take a nap to recharge.

More About Angels

Once you have identified how your angels communicate and are comfortable with them, you can talk to them at any time. Most angels don't stand on ceremony and come to you whenever you call for them or request their help. Sometimes, if they have a very important message for you, they may bring it to you during one of your regular meditations. It's wise to act on those messages as soon as possible as they seldom are about frivolous matters and oftentimes are a call for you to help someone or an animal in need.

It's good to know that most angels will not intervene in a situation unless you request them to, or if a parent or dependent asks on your behalf.

When communicating, angels can be quite obtuse, so feel free to ask questions and hope they reveal more.

If you're wondering what angels look like, they're most likely to look like what you'd expect or that you find non-threatening. This is because they don't like intimidating people. These days angels appear to people in meditation or physically in many forms and guises and take their cue on how to communicate from you.

***

For now, we invite you to continue experimenting and discovering more about meditation for yourself. Call on the angels for advice, protection, or companionship, and allow them to smooth the way for you to grow emotionally and into better health.

References

Black, D. S., O'Reilly, G. A., Olmstead, R., Breen, E. C., & Irwin, M. R. (2015). Mindfulness Meditation and improvement in sleep quality and daytime impairment among older adults with sleep disturbances. *JAMA Internal Medicine, 175*(4), 494. https://doi.org/10.1001/jamainternmed.2014.8081

Burke, A., Lam, C. N., Stussman, B., & Yang, H. (2017). Prevalence and patterns of use of mantra, mindfulness and spiritual meditation among adults in the United States. *BMC Complementary and Alternative Medicine, 17*(316). https://doi.org/10.1186/s12906-017-1827-8

D'Angelo Friedman, J. (2021, April 16). *How to use Mala Beads for meditation.* Yoga Journal. https://www.yogajournal.com/yoga-101/how-to-use-mala-beads-meditation/

de Lorent, L., Agorastos, A., Yassouridis, A., Kellner, M., & Muhtz, C. (2016). Auricular Acupuncture versus Progressive Muscle

Relaxation in patients with anxiety disorders or major depressive disorder: A prospective parallel group clinical trial. *Journal of Acupuncture and Meridian Studies*, *9*(4), 191–199. https://doi.org/10.1016/j.jams.2016.03.008

DiBenedetto, C. (2016, October 14). *5 Powerful mantras to help you quiet anxiety, beat self-doubt, manage stress, and more*. Health. https://www.health.com/mind-body/mantras-anxiety-confidence

Evans, J. (2012, October 17). *What is movement meditation? - AIHCP Health Care Blog*. AIHCP. https://aihcp.net/2012/10/17/what-is-movement-meditation/

Fletcher, E. (2015, September 10). *Why meditation & visualization aren't the same (and how to use them)*. Mindbodygreen. https://www.mindbodygreen.com/0-21539/why-meditation-visualization-arent-the-same-and-how-to-use-them.html

Grainger, C. (2018, August 8). *What is Mindful Movement and why should you try it?* The Sports Edit. https://thesportsedit.com/blogs/news/nutrition-what-is-mindful-movement

Hannay, C. (2021, December 14). *Mindful Teachers*. Mindful Teachers. https://www.mindfulteachers.org/blog/body-scan-and-progressive-relaxation

Heritage, S. (2014, March 1). *Transcendental meditation: does it work?* The Guardian. https://www.theguardian.com/lifeandstyle/2014/mar/01/transcendental-meditation-does-it-work

Higher self. (2022, March 21). Wikipedia. https://en.wikipedia.org/wiki/Higher_self

How to relax. (2018). Headspace; Headspace Inc. https://www.headspace.com/meditation/how-to-relax

James, A. (2019, April 9). *Focused Attention Vs. Open Awareness Meditation*. Pocket Mindfulness. https://www.pocketmindfulness.com/focused-open-meditation/

Khalsa, D. S. (2015). Stress, Meditation, and Alzheimer's disease prevention: Where the evidence stands. *Journal of Alzheimer's Disease, 48*(1), 1–12. https://doi.org/10.3233/jad-142766

Laz, A. (2020, October 5). *We're told to "connect to tur Higher Selves," but what does that really mean?* Mindbodygreen. https://www.mindbodygreen.com/articles/connect-to-your-higher-self-what-this-phrase-really-means/

Liu, K., Chen, Y., Wu, D., Lin, R., Wang, Z., & Pan, L. (2020). Effects of progressive muscle relaxation on anxiety and sleep quality in patients with COVID-19. *Complementary Therapies in Clinical Practice, 39,* 101132. https://doi.org/10.1016/j.ctcp.2020.101132

Loving-Kindness Meditation (Greater Good in Action). (n.d.). Ggia.berkeley.edu; Greater Good In Action. https://ggia.berkeley.edu/practice/loving_kindness_meditation

Draws on meditation by Eve Ekman

Loving-Kindness Meditation | The Buddhist Centre. (n.d.). Thebuddhistcentre.com. https://thebuddhistcentre.com/text/loving-kindness-meditation

Mayo Clinic. (2020, September 15). *Mindfulness exercises*. Mayo Clinic. https://www.mayoclinic.org/healthy-lifestyle/consumer-health/in-depth/mindfulness-exercises/art-20046356

Meyer, B., Keller, A., Wöhlbier, H.-G., Overath, C. H., Müller, B., & Kropp, P. (2016). Progressive muscle relaxation reduces migraine frequency and normalizes amplitudes of contingent negative variation (CNV). *The Journal of Headache and Pain, 17*(1). https://doi.org/10.1186/s10194-016-0630-0

Miller, B. (2022, May 10). *What is energy meditation? (with pictures)*. Www.wise-Geek.com. https://www.wise-geek.com/what-is-energy-meditation.htm#comments

Mindful. (2018). *Getting started with Mindfulness - Mindful*. Mindful. https://www.mindful.org/meditation/mindfulness-getting-started/

Mindful Staff. (2019, April 13). *How to meditate*. Mindful. https://www.mindful.org/how-to-meditate/

Mineo, L. (2018, April 17). *Less stress, clearer thoughts with mindfulness meditation*. Harvard Gazette; Harvard Gazette.

https://news.harvard.edu/gazette/story/2018/04/less-stress-clearer-thoughts-with-mindfulness-meditation/

Mitchell, J. T., McIntyre, E. M., English, J. S., Dennis, M. F., Beckham, J. C., & Kollins, S. H. (2013). A pilot trial of Mindfulness Meditation training for ADHD in adulthood: Impact on core symptoms, executive functioning, and emotion dysregulation. *Journal of Attention Disorders*, *21*(13), 1105–1120. https://doi.org/10.1177/1087054713513328

Mogeni, R., & Grebeniuk, I. (2020, December 7). *Spiritual Meditation: Discover the depths of who you are*. BetterMe Blog. https://betterme.world/articles/spiritual-meditation/

Nunez, K., & Minnis, G. (2020, August 10). *Progressive Muscle Relaxation: Benefits, how-to, technique*. Healthline. https://www.healthline.com/health/progressive-muscle-relaxation

Ong, J. C., Xia, Y., Smith-Mason, C. E., & Manber, R. (2018). A randomized controlled trial of Mindfulness Meditation for chronic insomnia: Effects on daytime symptoms and cognitive-emotional arousal. *Mindfulness*, *9*(6), 1702–1712. https://doi.org/10.1007/s12671-018-0911-6

Pearce, J. (2015, February 26). *5 Ways to connect with your guardian angel.* Mindbodygreen. https://www.mindbodygreen.com/0-17567/5-ways-to-connect-with-your-guardian-angel.html

Ponte Márquez, P. H., Feliu-Soler, A., Solé-Villa, M. J., Matas-Pericas, L., Filella-Agullo, D., Ruiz-Herrerias, M., Soler-Ribaudi, J., Roca-Cusachs Coll, A., & Arroyo-Díaz, J. A. (2018). Benefits of mindfulness meditation in reducing blood pressure and stress in patients with arterial hypertension. *Journal of Human Hypertension*, *33*(3), 237–247. https://doi.org/10.1038/s41371-018-0130-6

Porter, A., & Grebeniuk, I. (2020, July 8). *Moving Meditation: Reconciliation of body and mind.* BetterMe Blog. https://betterme.world/articles/moving-meditation/

Raypole, C. (2020, August 18). *Mantra meditation: Benefits, how to try it, and more.* Healthline. https://www.healthline.com/health/mantra-meditation

Raypole, C., & Legg, T. J. (2020a, March 26). *Body Scan Meditation: Benefits and how to do it.* Healthline. https://www.healthline.com/health/body-scan-meditation

Raypole, C., & Legg, T. J. (2020b, May 28). *Visualization Meditation: 5 Exercises to try.* Healthline. https://www.healthline.com/health/visualization-meditation

Riopel, L. (2019, November 28). *28 Best meditation techniques for beginners to learn.* PositivePsychology.com. https://positivepsychology.com/meditation-techniques-beginners/

Rollins, S. (2020, October 2). *The power of visualization: improve your skill by training your mind – Esports Healthcare.* Esportshealthcare.com; Esports Healthcare LLC. https://esportshealthcare.com/power-of-visualization/

Scott, E., & Clark, S. (2021, September 19). *How to practice focused meditation in just 30 minutes.* Verywell Mind. https://www.verywellmind.com/practice-focused-meditation-3144785#:~:text=Focused%20meditation%20involves%20focusing%20on

Stokes, V., & Sullivan, C. (2021, April 12). *Spiritual Meditation: What it is, benefits, and how to practice*. Healthline. https://www.healthline.com/health/mind-body/spiritual-meditation

Team, M. (2019, November 4). *What is Spiritual Meditation? - Keys to success & benefits [Video]*. Mindworks Meditation. https://mindworks.org/blog/what-is-spiritual-meditation/

Thorp, T. (2016, April 15). *How to use meditation to visualize your goals*. Chopra. https://chopra.com/articles/how-to-use-meditation-to-visualize-your-goals

Transcendental Meditation. (2020, December 22). Wikipedia. https://en.wikipedia.org/wiki/Transcendental_Meditation

What is the Higher Self? - Definition from Yogapedia. (n.d.). Yogapedia.com. Retrieved May 16, 2022, from https://www.yogapedia.com/definition/9304/higher-self

Wikipedia Contributors. (2019, February 25). *Meditation*. Wikipedia; Wikimedia Foundation. https://en.wikipedia.org/wiki/Meditation

Zeng, X., Chiu, C. P. K., Wang, R., Oei, T. P. S., & Leung, F. Y. K. (2015). The effect of loving-kindness meditation on positive emotions: a meta-analytic review. *Frontiers in Psychology*, 6. https://doi.org/10.3389/fpsyg.2015.01693

Images

Akyurt, Engin. *Woman in Black Top Sitting in Armchair*, 5 Dec. 2019, www.pexels.com/photo/woman-in-black-top-sitting-on-brown-armchair-3331574/.

Brothers Photo. "Sad Child Hugging Drawing," *Pexels.com*, 16 Nov. 2016, www.pexels.com/photo/monochrome-photo-of-sad-child-hugging-a-drawing-pad-240174/.

Comeau, Ezra. "Landscape Photography of Mountains and Water," *Pexels.com*, 7 June 2019, www.pexels.com/photo/landscape-photography-of-mountain-and-body-of-water-2387418/.

cottonbro. "Man with Red Jacket Sitting on Rock," *Pexels.com*, 17 Oct. 2020, www.pexels.com/photo/man-in-red-jacket-sitting-on-rock-5416318/.

Demidov, Alexey. "Brown and Red Beads," *Pexels.com*, 17 Feb. 2022, www.pexels.com/photo/brown-and-red-beaded-necklace-11215767/.

Designecologist. "Heart Shaped Red Neon," *Pexels.com*, 23 Feb. 2018, www.pexels.com/photo/heart-shaped-red-neon-signage-887349/.

Fairytale, Elina. "Lavender and Massage Oils," *Pexels.com*, 23 Mar. 2020, www.pexels.com/photo/lavender-and-massage-oils-3865676/.

Karpovich, Vlada. "Elderly Couple Meditating in Park," *Pexels.com*, 28 July 2021, www.pexels.com/photo/an-elderly-couple-meditating-in-the-park-8940499/.

KoolShooters. "A Man and Woman Dressed as Angels," *Pexels.com*, June 2021, www.pexels.com/photo/a-man-and-woman-wearing-angel-costumes-8513040/.

Mack, Ben. "Anonymous Woman on Beach," *Pexels.com*, 27 Oct. 2020, www.pexels.com/photo/anonymous-woman-on-beach-with-rainbow-5708071/.

Nguyen, Pew. "Signage," *Pexels.com*, 26 Nov. 2016, www.pexels.com/photo/signage-241028/.

Nilov, Mikhail. "Man in Green and Black," *Pexels.com*, 21 Feb. 2021, www.pexels.com/photo/light-man-people-woman-6932056/.

---. "Red and Yellow Flower," *Pexels.com*, 24 Feb. 2021, www.pexels.com/photo/red-and-yellow-flower-in-bloom-6932130/.

Otto, Noelle. "Woman in Brown Sleeveless Dress," *Pexels.com*, 29 Mar. 2018, www.pexels.com/photo/woman-in-brown-sleeveless-dress-and-blue-jeans-standing-on-gray-path-road-906106/.

Pauccara, Hernan. "Frozen Wave against Sun," *Pexels.com*, July 2018, www.pexels.com/photo/frozen-wave-against-sunlight-1210273/.

Pixabay. "Light Painting at Night," *Pexels.com*, 30 Sept. 2017, www.pexels.com/photo/light-painting-at-night-327509/.

Shvets, Anna. "Person Leaning on Table," *Pexels.com*, 27 Oct. 2020, Photo www.pexels.com/photo/photo-of-person-leaning-on-the-table-with-ceramic-figurines-5682166/.

Syrikova, Tatiana. "Wigwam Placed on Terrace," *Pexels.com*, 22 May 2020, www.pexels.com/photo/wigwam-placed-on-wooden-terrace-with-picturesque-view-3932976/.

Turnell, Ian. "Body of Water between Green Leafy Trees," *Pexels.com*, 2 Dec. 2017, www.pexels.com/photo/body-of-water-between-green-leaf-trees-709552/.

Wheeler, James. "Pathway Surrounded by Fir Trees," *Pexels.com*, 8 Nov. 2018, www.pexels.com/photo/photo-of-pathway-surrounded-by-fir-trees-1578750/.

www.ingramcontent.com/pod-product-compliance
Lightning Source LLC
Chambersburg PA
CBHW050318010526
44107CB00055B/2291